F-14 TOMCAT
in action

By Al Adcock

Color by Don Greer

Illustrated by Perry Manley

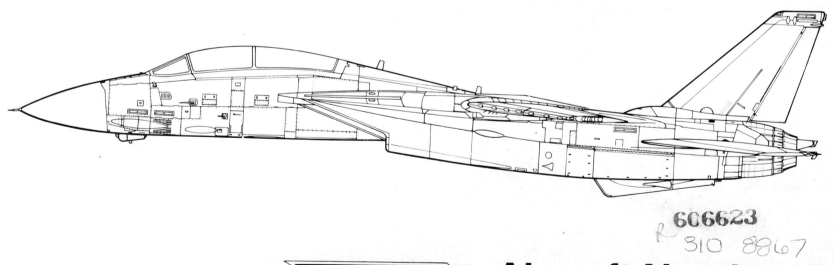

Aircraft Number 105

squadron/signal publications

On 4 January 1989, two Libyan MiG-23 Floggers engaged two F-14A Tomcats of VF-32 flying from USS JOHN F. KENNEDY over the Mediterranean. The Tomcats shot both aircraft down, after repeatedly trying to evade the Libyan fighters and avoid a shooting incident.

ISBN 0-89747-247-0

If you have any photographs of the aircraft, armor, soldiers or ships of any nation, particularly wartime snapshots, why not share them with us and help make Squadron/Signal's books all the more interesting and complete in the future. Any photograph sent to us will be copied and the original returned. The donor will be fully credited for any photos used. Please send them to:

Squadron/Signal Publications, Inc.
1115 Crowley Drive.
Carrollton, TX 75011-5010.

Dedication

To all Naval Aviators — Past, Present and Future

Acknowledgements

I want to thank Lois Lovisolo at the Grumman History Center, Bethpage, New York for all of her help. Without her assistance this book would have been impossible to complete. Two other persons at Grumman were also of great help: Bill Ennis (F-14 Program Customer Relations Manager) and Pete Kirkup (Assistant Curator, Grumman History Center). Many Thanks to you all.

Photo Credits

CDR Gus Grissom, Jr.	LT Bruce Kissick
Grumman Aerospace	Russell D. Egnor
U.S. Navy	Nancy Lovato
NASA	Fran Slimmer
Hughes Aircraft	Ed Keller
General Dynamics	Commodore Marty P. Morgen
General Electric	Clifton Bushey
McDonnell-Douglas	Tim Beecher
Northrop	Maria T. Oharenko
USAF Armament Museum	LT Joseph M. Mizerak
Loral Corporation	Bill Johnson
Candid Aero-Files	Jim Presley
Mike Slover	Howard Corns
VF-31	LT Mark Wilcox
VF-142	Elizabeth Kral
VF-211	VF-11
VF-74	VF-103
David F. Brown	Harry Gann
William C. Barto	Chuck Porter

An overall Light Gull Gray F-14A Tomcat of VF-142 on patrol over the Atlantic Ocean. The squadron was assigned to Carrier Air Wing 7 aboard the nuclear powered carrier USS DWIGHT D. EISENHOWER (CVN-69). (USN via LT J. Mizerak)

INTRODUCTION

Since the earliest days of carrier aviation, air cover for the fleet has been provided by air superiority fighters, a great number of which have been built by the Grumman Aircraft Engineering Corporation.

Grumman was formed on 6 December 1928, with total capital of $64,000.00. The company was founded by Leroy Randle Grumman and five other aeronautical engineers and businessmen. Their early designs were innovative and included the first military aircraft with retractable landing gear and the first military float plane with its own retractable landing gear (creating a new class of aircraft — the amphibian). Grumman's design for the folding wing (later to be called the sto-wing) that reduced the span of the folded wing to that of the horizontal stabilizer, made it possible to carry more aircraft on a carrier. These and other innovations placed Grumman in the forefront of U.S. Navy aircraft production during the 1930s. When the Second World War began, Grumman shifted to full scale war production and during the war 31,376 Grumman aircraft were produced. 17,573 were built by Grumman and 13,803 by the General Motors Eastern Aircraft Division, which produced the FM-1, FM-2, TBM and some 330 J2F-3 Ducks under license.

After the Second World War, designers began concentrating on turbojet powered aircraft. German aeronautical engineers, particularly at Messerschmitt, had been investigating variable sweep wings and had built a prototype, the P1101. The P1101 was an experimental turbojet fighter, using both aluminum and wood (for non-load carrying fuselage and wing components) in its construction. The P1101 featured a low mounted Junkers Jumo axial flow turbojet and had the variable sweep wings mounted high on the fuselage. The wings of the P1101 could be set on the ground for a sweep of from 35 to 45 degrees.

The P1101 prototype never flew, and on 29 April 1945, the Messerschmitt research facility at Oberammergan was captured by American troops. The aircraft and all research records were impounded and sent to the United States. Little interest was shown in the data until Robert Wood of Bell Aircraft saw the possibilities of the variable sweep wing and persuaded Bell and NACA (National Advisory Committee on Aeronautics) to fund a research project based on the German data. The P1101 airframe was provided to Bell to serve as the basis for the Bell X-5 (the X-5 actually used various components from the P1101 airframe) and the first (of two) X-5s flew on 20 June 1951. With a wing that could be varied from 20 to 60 degress in flight, the X-5 program provided NACA with a great deal of data on variable sweep wings.

Grumman engineers felt that the variable geometry wing had great potential for carrier based fighters. Their first project, the Grumman XF10F-1 Jaguar, featured a wing that could be moved forty degrees while in flight. The XF10F-1 was a very large fighter, weighing 33,000 pounds and having a fifty foot seven inch wing span (at minimum sweep). The Jaguar was powered by a 11,600 lbst Westinghouse J40-WE-8 afterburning turbojet which gave it a top speed of 722 mph. The XF10F-1 flew for the first time on 19 May 1953 and flight testing revealed problems that eventually caused the project to be cancelled (although prior to its first flight the Navy had ordered thirty aircraft).

The shipboard fleet air defense fighter throughout the 1960s was the McDonnell-Douglas F-4 Phantom II. The F-4 was designed as a carrier based fleet defense fighter carrying a complement of long range air-to-air missiles and deleting the gun armament. During the Vietnam War, the lack of a gun proved to be a problem once the Phantoms became engaged in air-to-air combat with North Vietnamese Air Force (NVAF) MiG-17 and MiG-19 fighters, both of which had gun armament.

This mock-up is of Grumman's Model 303-F, a forerunner to the F-14 which featured a single vertical stabilizer. The design was not chosen because of its weight, carrier hangar deck space considerations and projections that it would have poor low altitude performance. (Grumman)

When a replacement for the Republic F-105 was being considered by the USAF, the Secretary of Defense, Robert McNamara, decided to combine the needs of both services and purchase one aircraft capable of meeting those needs. The Navy was looking for a carrier based fleet defense fighter to replace the F-4, a far cry from the strike fighter replacement the USAF wanted. The combined program was known as the TFX or Tactical Fighter Experimental. The design that was accepted by the USAF and USN became the F-111. Two variants were to be built, one by General Dynamics (F-111A) and one by Grumman (sub-contractor to General Dynamics) as the Navy F-111B. When the gross catapult weight of the F-111B exceeded 77,500 pounds (up from a design weight of 62,788 pounds), Grumman engineers knew that the Navy would reject the F-111B.

To replace the F-111B, Grumman proposed its design G-303 to the Navy during 1967. Grumman's G-303 incorporated a number of features from the F-111B project, including the variable sweep wing, Hughes AWG-9 radar fire control system, Hughes AIM-54 Phoenix missiles and the Pratt and Whitney TF-30-P-1 turbofan engines. Grumman's first proposal, the G-303-60, had podded engines and a high mounted variable sweep wing. During the course of refining the design, seven different versions were proposed, from the 303-F which had a fixed high wing, to the 303-E which emerged as the prototype for the F-14.

Experience with the F-111B convinced the Navy that they needed an aircraft designed to meet their needs and, in July of 1968, a request for proposals was issued to U.S. aircraft manufacturers. The proposal submitted by Grumman was accepted and a contract was signed during February of 1968 for six prototype/pre-production aircraft under the designation F-14A. These aircraft were assigned BuNos 157980 through 157985. The first prototype XF-14A (BuNo 157980) made its first flight on 21 December 1970, just twenty-one months after the original contract was signed.

The prototype's first flight was short and uneventful; however, the second flight ended with the loss of the aircraft. A backup hydraulic pump failed and the leaking fluid caused the primary system to fail. Unable to maintain control, the crew was forced to eject, just short of the Calverton runway. Soon after the loss of the prototype, the Navy contracted for an additional six pre-production aircraft (BuNos 157986-157991). Grumman produced twelve pre-production F-14As, and replaced the Number 1 prototype aircraft with the Number 12 aircraft, calling BuNo 157991 Aircraft 1X and giving it the first prototype's BuNo (157980).

The XF-14A prototype (BuNo 157980) during its successful first test flight. On the aircraft's second flight, a failed hydraulic pump caused the total loss of flight controls and the XF-14A crashed short of the Calverton runway after the crew safely ejected. (Grumman)

This pre-production F-14A (aircraft number 10, BuNo 167989) carries Black photographic reference stripes on the fuselage. Aircraft number 10 was used for flight tests to determine the flight envelope of the F-14A and was later lost while conducting spin tests. (Grumman)

Pre-production aircraft number 11 was demonstrated to U.S. Congressmen aboard USS INDEPENDENCE during 1972 to prove the Tomcat's suitability for carrier service. Aircraft number 11 carried the standard Navy Light Gull Gray over White camouflage scheme with Insignia Red bands on the ventral fin, vertical fin, horizontal stabilizers and wing tips. (Grumman)

The F-14A prototype pioneered the use of exotic materials in aircraft construction. The horizontal stabilizer skin was the first production component of any aircraft, civilian or military, made of composites. The F-14A made extensive use of titanium (24.4 percent), aluminum alloy (39.4 percent) and steel (17.4 percent). The swing wing design, although making the airframe heavier, enabled the F-14A to take off in less than 1,000 feet and land in less than 2,000 feet, at speeds below 120 mph. The F-14As were powered by two 20,900 lbst Pratt and Whitney TF-30-P12 turbofan engines. These engines gave the prototype a top speed of Mach 2.4 (with the wings fully swept back to 68 degrees).

The prototype had a length of sixty-two feet and a span of sixty-four feet one and one half inches with wings full forward and thirty-eight feet two and one quarter inches with the wings swept back. The wings could be swept back (on the ground) some 75 degrees for carrier storage. This over-sweep feature reduces the span to thirty-three feet three inches. The prototype weighed 40,070 pounds empty and had a gross weight (maximum catapult weight) of 72,000 pounds.

The aircraft's internal armament was a 20MM M61 General Electric Vulcan cannon capable of firing up to 6,000 rounds a minute. Total capacity of the ammunition drum was 675 rounds. Externally, various air-to-air missiles could be carried, including the AIM-54A Phoenix, AIM-7 Sparrow and AIM-9 Sidewinder.

During 1971, Grumman made a proposal to the USAF to use the F-14A for its Improved Manned Interceptor (IMI) program. The IMI program was aimed at finding a replacement for the Convair F-106 and since the F-14A could fulfill the majority of the specifications, a mock-up was built using the 303-E wooden mock-up as a base. In the event, the McDonnell-Douglas F-15 was selected to replace the F-106. Also during 1971, the Navy asked McDonnell-Douglas to design a shipboard variant of the F-15 (F-15N) for testing against the F-14A. The increased weight, cost and greatly reduced performance of the F-15N quickly killed the project.

During late 1971, a contract was issued by the Naval Air Systems Command for 301 production F-14A aircraft (the contract also included the twelve pre-producion aircraft) and the Grumman Iron Works was back in the Naval fighter business after having been absent from carrier decks for twelve years.

Development

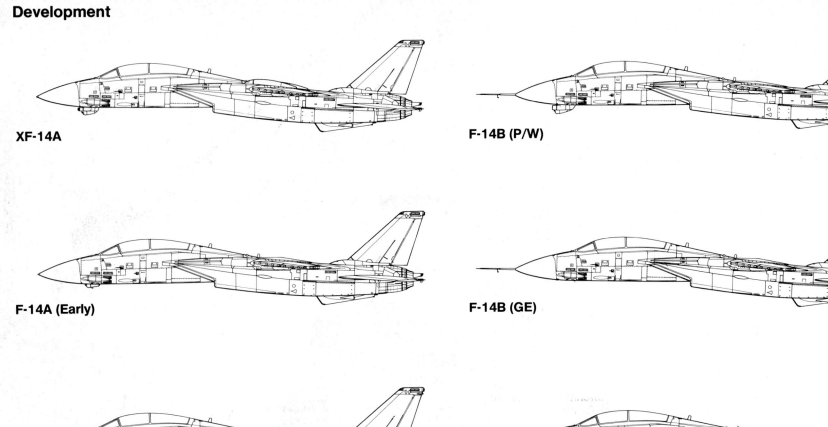

XF-14A

F-14B (P/W)

F-14A (Early)

F-14B (GE)

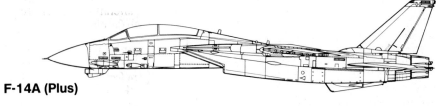

F-14A (Late)

F-14A (Plus)

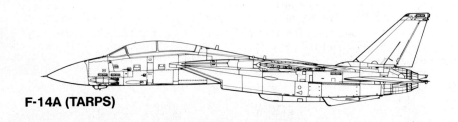

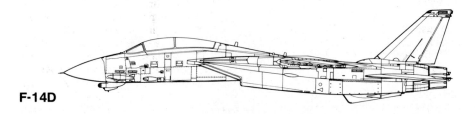

F-14A (TARPS)

F-14D

F-14A

The production F-14A differed very little from the prototype/pre-production F-14As with the exception of the under nose chin electronics pod and the rear fuselage area. Shortly after production began, the rear fuselage "beaver tail" was reconfigured to improve subsonic cruise performance and combat radius. The change went through three stages: the original configuration, an interim configuration, and the final production configuration. The interim change was installed on aircraft number eighty-six and was retrofitted to earlier aircraft at Naval Rework Facilities during scheduled overhauls. The production change went into effect with aircraft number eighty-seven.

During this change, the shape of the air brakes was also modified, the rear position light was moved from the "boat tail" to the tip of the port vertical fin, and the starboard chaff/flare dispenser was moved to be alongside the port dispenser.

Production F-14As have also been noted with several different style under nose sensor pods. Some pods house ECM gear and an infrared sensor, others house just the ECM gear, while still others house just an infrared sensor. F-14s have also been noted with no pod being carried.

Late production F-14As (Block 95 and later) have had the nose modified with the addition of a short pitot tube mounted on the extreme end of the radome. Additionally, the under nose sensor pod on late production F-14As carries the Northrop developed Television Camera Set (TCS). The TCS optical unit is housed in the chin pod and when carrying the TCS, the infrared seeker/ECM is mounted below the optical unit.

The TCS unit enables the aircrew to track and identify enemy aircraft beyond visual range (normally two-three miles). In some cases, crews have reported being able to visually identify aircraft with the TCS at ranges in excess of nine miles. The TV pictures are also stored on video tape by a video cassette recorder called the Tactical Data Recording System (TDRS). The TCS can be slaved to the aircraft radar and will automatically search, acquire and lock on to distant targets detected by the aircraft's radar. The black and white video pictures are displayed on video screens in both the pilot and radar intercept officer's (RIO) cockpits.

The production F-14A had an overall length (including pitot tube) of sixty-two feet eight inches, a wing span of thirty-eight feet two and one half inches (swept) or sixty-four feet one and one half inches (unswept) and a height of sixteen feet. The wing's angle of sweep can be varied from 20 to 68 degrees in flight and for deck storage the wing can be over swept to 75 degrees, reducing the wing span to that of the horizontal stabilizers. A wing glove extends from the upper air intake fairing when the wings are fully swept and the aircraft is at speeds exceeding Mach 1. The wing glove compensates for aerodynamic forces and are manually controlled below Mach 1 and computer controlled above Mach 1. Empty weight is 40,104 pounds, gross weight with six Phoenix missiles is 70,599 pounds and maximum weight is 74,349 pounds. The landing weight is set at 51,830 pounds.

Production F-14As, like the prototype/pre-production aircraft, are powered by two 20,900 lbst Pratt and Whitney TF30 afterburning turbofan engines. Early production aircraft used the P&W TF30-P-412A, while late production aircraft were fitted with improved TF30-P-414A. In full afterburner, the F-14A has a maximum speed of Mach 2.4 (1,544 mph), while normal cruising speed is 400-500 knots. The Tomcat's landing speed is 122 knots, with wings at the 20 degree setting and stall speed is 103 knots.

The heart of the F-14A weapons system is the Hughes AWG-9 fire control system. This system consists of a pulse Doppler radar with a look-down capability and a fire control computer. With an effective search range of over 170 nautical miles on narrow scan,

Tomcat 614 (BuNo 158614) comes to a halt after making an arrested landing aboard USS FORRESTAL (CV-59). After the deck crew disengaged the arresting cable, the F-14 taxied into position for another launch. F-14A (BuNo 158613), in the foreground, is carrying an inert AIM-54 Phoenix on the wing pylon. (Grumman)

the radar can spot approaching targets long before the F-14 can be detected. The AWG-9 system can track twenty-four targets at the same time and fire six AIM-54 Phoenix air-to-air missiles simultaneously engaging six different targets. The Tomcat is also equipped with UHF and VHF radios, an Identification Friend or Foe (IFF) transponder and a Kaiser Vertical Head Up Display (HUD).

Internal armament for the F-14A is the General Electric M61-A1 Vulcan 20MM six barrel cannon with a rate of fire of up to 6,000 rounds per minute. The weapon is fed cased ammunition from a 675 round capacity ammunition drum in the lower fuselage, under the cockpit, by a flexible chute. The F-14A has provisions for six AIM-54 Phoenix missiles (either A, B or C series) plus two AIM-9 Sidewinders air-to-air missiles (either G, H or L series). Alternate missile loads include four Phoenix, two AIM-7F Sparrows and two Sidewinders, or six AIM-7F Sparrows and two Sidewinders, or four AIM-7M Sparrows and four Sidewinders.

As production got underway at Grumman, the Navy was completing carrier suitability trials for the Tomcat aboard USS FORRESTAL (CV-59) proving that the F-14A was fully carrier capable. Missile handling and firing trials were successfully conducted by the Naval Missile Center (now the Pacific Missile Test Center) Point Mugu, California, and

F-14A Number 12 (BuNo 158616) was used for catapult tests at the Naval Air Test Center, Pax River, Maryland, during 1972. The tests included launches at various weights and with various missiles carried on the wing pylons. The aircraft carries a Red identification band on the nose and Black photographic reference stripes on the fuselage. (USN)

A deck crewman removes the nose wheel tow bar from aircraft number 11 during carrier suitability trials aboard USS INDEPENDENCE (CV-62) during March of 1972. The aircraft is carrying dummy Sparrow missiles in the underfuselage missile bays. (Grumman)

the Naval Air Test Center (NATC) at Patuxent River, Maryland, clearing the Tomcat's weapons system for service use.

Deliveries of production F-14As to the Fleet began in June of 1972. The Pacific Fleet Readiness Squadron, VF-124, was the first to receive the Tomcat. VF-124, based at Naval Air Station Mirimar, San Diego, California, was responsible for training both flight and ground crews for operational squadrons. Two operational squadrons were established to introduce the F-14A into the fleet. Fighter Squadron One (VF-1) and Fighter Squadron Two (VF-2) were officially re-established (both units were prior USN squadrons that had been deactivated) on 14 October 1972 at NAS Mirimar. After a period of intensive training and work-ups, the squadrons made their initial deployment aboard USS ENTERPRISE (CVN-65) during September of 1974.

With the ENTERPRISE deployment, the F-14A was declared fully operational. The Tomcat's first combat missions were flown by VF-1 and VF-2 during the U.S. evacuation of Saigon. Operation FREQUENT WIND, conducted during late April of 1975, removed the last Americans from South Vietnam and Tomcat crews flew Combat Air Patrol (CAP) missions to protect the Fleet. The North Vietnamese Air Force, however, decided not to interfere with the carriers and the F-14 crews did not get the chance to test their new mounts in combat.

The first Atlantic Fleet deployment of the F-14A was aboard USS JOHN F. KENNEDY (CV-67) during June of 1975. Fighter Squadron Fourteen (VF-14) and Fighter Squadron Thirty-two (VF-32) were assigned to the ship as part of Carrier Air Wing Three, the second oldest Navy Air Wing. The highly successful cruise was completed during January of 1976, after serving six months with the 6th Fleet in the Mediterranean Sea.

In operational service, the F-14A performs three missions: long range intercept, Combat Air Patrol (CAP) and Barrier Combat Air Patrol (BARCAP). Additionally, Tomcats are maintained on Five Minute Alert status (known as the Alert Five), acting as a deck launched interceptor (DLI) to counter intruders that approach the Fleet or aircraft that get through the outer screen of patrolling Tomcats. As a long range interceptor, the F-14A normally carries an armament of six AIM-54 Phoenix missiles. For short range missions, four Phoenix, two AIM-7 Sparrows and two AIM-9 Sidewinder would be carried. For BARCAP missions, either four Sparrows and four Sidewinders or six AIM-120 AMRAAM missiles would be carried.

The F-14A is also capable of air-to-ground missions, although this is not a normal role for the Tomcat. For this role, the F-14 has the capability of carrying up to fourteen Mk 82 500 pound bombs, or eight Mk 83 1,000 pound bombs, or four Mk 84 2,000 pound bombs. Bombs and Sidewinder missiles can be carried in combination, up to a maximum external load of 14,500 pounds.

As part of the ongoing F-14 update program, the Sparrow missile will eventually be replaced by the Hughes AIM-120A AMRAAM (Advanced Medium Range Air-to-Air Missile). The AMRAAM is about one third the weight of an AIM-7 Sparrow and has a greater range and larger warhead. Another missile scheduled for clearance for the F-14A is the Texas Instruments AGM-88A HARM (High Speed Anti-Radiation Missile). HARM has been operational since December of 1982 and was used by the A-6s and A-7s against Libyan SA-5 radar sites during Operation EL DORADO CANYON, on 24 March 1985. HARM uses a sophisticated seeker and autopilot to detect, identify and home in on hostile radars.

The F-14A is equipped with various Electronic Counter Measures (ECM) equipment such as the AN/ALE-39 Chaff and Flare dispenser. The dispenser is located in the lower portion of the rear fuselage underside. The unit can dispense chaff, flares and various other jammer cartridges within the E/G/I frequency bands. Normally, one dispenser is loaded on the F-14A, although there is provision for a second dispenser.

Two different style external fuel tanks can be carried on the F-14A. One tank has no fins and has a capacity of 270 gallons, while the second style is equipped with fins and has a capacity of 267 gallons. The finned tank is used only on the F-14A, while the finless tank can be used either on the F-14A or the F-14A (Plus). The finned tank is currently being phased out, since it was found to cause a slight buffet as the F-14 approached transonic speeds.

The versatility of the F-14A has been further increased with the addition of a TARPS (Tactical Aerial Reconnaissance Pod System) pod under the fuselage of specially modified F-14As. There are currently forty-seven F-14As in service that are capable of carrying the TARPS. The system was designed to give the Navy an interim tactical photographic reconnaissance capability (lost when the RA-5C Vigilante was retired) until the dedicated RF-18 Hornet enters fleet service. TARPS is seventeen feet long and is carried on fuselage weapons station five. The pod contains three sensors and their associated equipment. The sensors carried include a two position KS-87B framing camera for forward oblique and vertical photography, a 9 inch focal length high-resolution KA-99A low/medium altitude panoramic camera and an AAD-5A infrared line scan system. The pod's environmental control system (ECS) uses cooling air supplied from the carrying aircraft, in much the same manner as the AIM-54 Phoenix missile.

With the TARPS pod in place, the F-14A still maintains its offensive and defensive weapons capability since only weapons station five is occupied by TARPS. Under normal circumstances, three aircraft within a VF squadron (usually the number two squadron within the Air Wing) are TARPS equipped. The first TARPS deployment was with Fighter Squadron Eighty-four (VF-84) aboard USS NIMITZ (CVN-68).

Chin Pods

XF-14A Prototype

Infrared Seeker

Anti-Collision Light

ALQ-100 ECM Antenna

F-14A (Early)

Anti-collision Light

ALQ-100/126 ECM Antenna

An F-14A (BuNo 157988) of the Naval Missile Center (NMC) fires an AIM-54A Phoenix during early weapons testing. The AIM-54 has a range of over 100 miles, giving the F-14 the greatest stand-off engagement range of any fighter in the world. An F-14A can carry up to six AIM-54s and the AWG-9 can guide all six to individual targets at the same time. (USN)

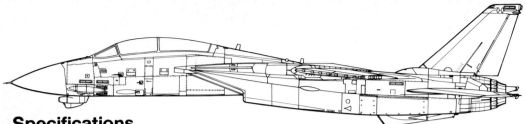

Specifications
Grumman F-14A Tomcat

Wingspan .64 feet 1 ½ inches (unswept)
38 feet 2 ½ inches (swept)
Length . . . . .62 feet 8 inches
Height . . . . .16 feet
Empty Weight . . . . .40,104 pounds
Maximum Weight . . . . .74,349 pounds
Powerplants . . . . .Two Pratt & Whitney 20,900 lbst
TF-30-P-414A turbofan engines

Armament . . . . .One M61-A1 20мм cannon
(internal), six AIM-54
Phoenix or six AIM-7 Sparrow
missiles and two
AIM-9 Sidewinder missiles.

Performance
  Maximum Speed . . . . .1,544 mph
  Service ceiling . . . . .50,000 feet
  Range . . . . .2,000 miles (with tanks)
Crew . . . . .Two

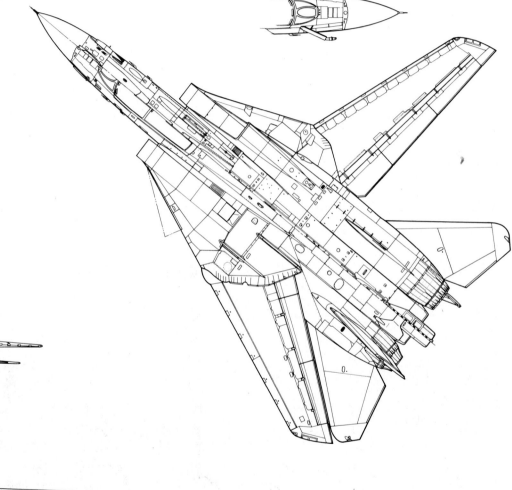

The first operational F-14A squadron was VF-1 Wolfpack based at Naval Air Station Miramar, California. VF-1 (and VF-2) was recommissioned during 1972 specifically to introduce the F-14A to the fleet. VF-1 saw action aboard USS ENTERPRISE (CVN-65) during the April 1975 evacuation of South Vietnam, known as Operation FREQUENT WIND. (USN)

An F-14A of VF-2 Bounty Hunters, the second F-14A squadron, takes a wave-off from the LSO aboard USS ENTERPRISE (CVN-65). On this cruise VF-2 (also known as the Bullets) was awarded a Meritorious Unit Commendation for its outstanding performance while deployed to the Western Pacific (WESTPAC). (USN)

A section of early production F-14As of VF-1 Wolfpack on patrol above the Pacific during the mid-1970s. These aircraft are fitted with the modified beaver tail first introduced on aircraft eighty-six. This modification was retrofitted to earlier Tomcats during their regular overhaul. (USN)

This F-14A (BuNo 160380) was assigned to VF-84 Jolly Rogers aboard USS NIMITZ (CVN-68) during 1978. The squadron was attached to Carrier Air Wing Eight (CVW-8) for deployment to the Mediterranean Sea. VF-84 markings consisted of a White skull and crossbones on a Black background. The AJ tail code is Black outlined in White, while the fuselage stripe is Dark Blue with Yellow outline and triangles. (USN)

An F-14A (BuNo 158629) of VF-124 Gunfighters on the ramp at NAS Miramar, California. VF-124 is the Pacific Replacement Air Group (RAG) responsible for training F-14 air and ground crews for the Pacific area. VF-124's tail markings are Red and White. (INTERAIR)

"Beaver" Tails

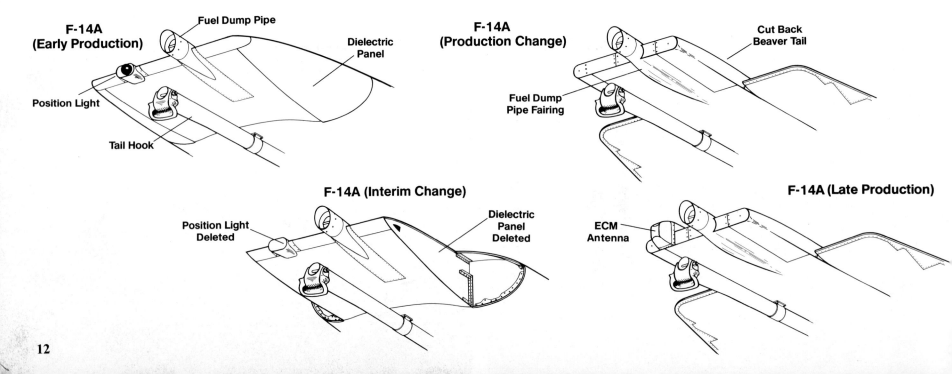

F-14A (Early Production)
- Fuel Dump Pipe
- Dielectric Panel
- Position Light
- Tail Hook

F-14A (Production Change)
- Cut Back Beaver Tail
- Fuel Dump Pipe Fairing

F-14A (Interim Change)
- Position Light Deleted
- Dielectric Panel Deleted

F-14A (Late Production)
- ECM Antenna

An F-14A (BuNo 159849) of VF-114 Aardvarks on the ramp at NAS Miramar, California, during late 1977. A Foreign Object Damage (FOD) screen is in place over the starboard intake while the port screen is visible just behind the nosewheel. The Aardvark, fuselage stripe, and tips of the vertical stabilizers are Orange. (INTERAIR)

An F-14A of VF-14 Tophatters off the USS KENNEDY escorts a Tu-16 Badger D maritime/electronic reconnaissance bomber of the Soviet Naval Air Force over the Atlantic during November of 1976. The Badger was attempting to shadow naval units engaged in Operation TEAMWORK, a combined NATO exercise. (USN by LTJG Nagelin)

This section of F-14As of VF-32 Swordsmen was stationed aboard the USS JOHN F. KENNEDY (CV-67) for a brief period from June of 1975 to January of 1976 for the Tomcat's first Atlantic cruise. The Black anti-glare panel is unusual in that it extends well to the rear of the cockpit along the fuselage spine. (USN)

13

These F-14As of VF-211 Fighting Checkmates aboard USS CONSTELLATION (CV-64) were attached to Carrier Air Wing Nine (CVW-9) during 1978. The squadron markings consist of Red and White checkerboards on the outboard rudders, with Red, White and Blue stripes on the top and bottom of the vertical stabilizers. (USN)

This F-14A of VF-211 Fighting Checkmates served with CVW-9 aboard USS CONSTELLATION (CV-64) during May of 1989. The Tomcat carries Red and White checkered rudders and Red, White and Blue stripes on the vertical stabilizers. (USN)

A Yellow shirted plane director signals an F-14A of VF-114 Aardvarks to hold as the catapult launch bar is positioned in the shuttle. VF-114 shared the deck with their sister squadron VF-213 Black Lions aboard USS KITTY HAWK (CV-63) operating in the Philippine Sea. (USN)

Position Light

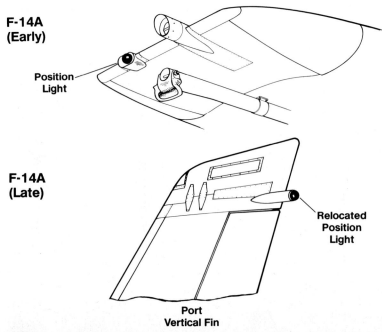

F-14A
(Early)

Position
Light

F-14A
(Late)

Relocated
Position
Light

Port
Vertical Fin

Navy tactical aircraft have had their markings toned down to make them less visible in the air. This F-14A (BuNo 160930) of VF-124 Gunfighters at NAS Miramar carries a camouflage of overall Flat Gull Gray. While the warning markings and national insignia are in color, all other markings are in Black. (INTERAIR)

This F-14A (BuNo 161860) of VF-31 Tomcatters is armed with AIM-7 Sparrow and AIM-9 Sidewinder air-to-air missiles. The Black nosed F-14A is finished in overall Light Gull Gray with a Red tail, Black AE code on the inside of the vertical stabilizers, and the Felix the Cat insignia on the fin. (USN)

An F-14A of VF-41 Black Aces prepares for launch with the nose tow bar in the catapult shuttle and the hold back bar in place. The Black Aces made the first combat kill by an F-14 during 1981 when two VF-41 Tomcats shot down two Lybian Sukhoi Su-22 Fitters over the Gulf of Sidra. (USN by LT Bill Linder)

This F-14A of VF-111 Sundowners flies over the Pacific off the island of Oahu, Hawaii, during April of 1981. The Tomcat carries AIM-9 Sidewinder air-to-air missiles on the wing pylons. The Sundowners completed their transition from the F-4 Phantom during April of 1979. (USN via LT Pittman)

This F-14A (BuNo 159006, AB-103) is attached to VF-102 Diamondbacks as part of Carrier Air Wing One aboard USS AMERICA (CV-66). The fuselage stripes, wing glove markings, diamond outline and tail code are in Red. During the 1986 raid on Libya, the Diamondbacks provided combat air patrols over the fleet. (USN by Robert S. Lawson)

The speed brakes are fully deployed and the landing gear is extended; however, the tailhook is retracted as this F-14A of VF-101 Grim Reapers executes a go-around during a training mission. VF-101 is the Atlantic Fleet Replacement Air Group (RAG). (USN)

Upper Speed Brake

F-14A (Early)

F-14A (Late)

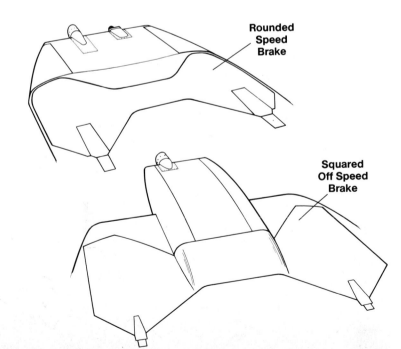

Rounded Speed Brake

Squared Off Speed Brake

Aircraft of Carrier Air Wing Fourteen (CVW-14) on the deck of USS CONSTELLATION (CV-64) during 1984. The fighter component of the air wing consisted of VF-21 and VF-164. The Air Wing was participating in Fleet Exercise 85, which was the first time F-14As and the F/A-18s operated from the same carrier. (USN by M. Tamberg)

An F-14A of VF-21 Freelancers comes to a halt on the angle deck of USS CONSTELLATION (CV-64). The White dots on the deck are tie-down locations and the vehicle in the foreground is an MD-3A tow vehicle modified for fire fighting duties. (USN via M. Tamberg)

An F-14A of VF-103 Sluggers catches a wire aboard USS SARATOGA (CV-60) during 1986. VF-103 F-14As carry an S on the fin signifying a safety award for six years and 18,500 accident free flying hours. VF-103 transitioned from the F-4S Phantom to the F-14A Tomcat during January of 1983. (USN via W Shayka)

A section of F-14As of VF-211 Fighting Checkmates escort a Tu-95 Bear G electronic warfare aircraft of the Soviet Navy over the South China Sea during 1986. The Bear was operating out of the old US base at Cam Rhan Bay, Vietnam, which was being used as a Soviet naval and air base. (LT Butch Kissick USN)

A TARPS equipped F-14A (BuNo 161273) of VF-2 Bounty Hunters escorts an A-6 Intruder of VA-145 Swordsmen, armed with an AGM-88A Harm anti-radiation missile during a photographic mission. Both aircraft are with CVW-2 aboard USS KITTY HAWK (CV-63). (Grumman)

An F-14A of VF-11 Red Rippers engages the number 3 wire for a perfect arrested landing aboard USS FORRESTAL (CV-59) in the Mediterranean Sea with the U.S. Sixth Fleet. The tips of the vertical stabilizers are Red and the anti-glare panel is Dark Blue-Gray. (USN)

A pair of F-14A Tomcats of VF-41 Black Aces on combat air patrol over the Mediterranean Sea during 1986. AJ-111 and 113 are both armed with AIM-9 Sidewinder and AIM-7 Sparrow air-to-air missiles and are equipped with 270 gallon fuel tanks. The wing gloves are extended indicating that the aircraft are approaching Mach 1. (USN by R. Beno)

This F-14A of VF-84 Jolly Rogers is finished in three tone tactical camouflage consisting of Light Gull Gray vertical stabilizers, Medium Flat Gray fuselage uppersurfaces over Gull Gray undersurfaces. The Tomcat was stationed aboard USS NIMITZ (CVN-68) during 1986. (USN by R. Beno)

An F-14A of VF-51 Screaming Eagles tied down on the deck of the USS CARL VINSON (CVN-70) during December of 1984. The VINSON was operating in the Sea of Japan conducting exercises with the Japanese. The Tomcat has a tow bar attached to the nosewheel indicating that it is one of the alert fighters. (Alan Robertson)

Hook down, an F-14A of VF-142 Ghostriders turns onto final approach for landing aboard USS DWIGHT D. EISENHOWER (CVN-69) in the Mediterranean Sea. The aircraft is armed with two AIM-9 Sidewinders and two AIM-54 Phoenix air-to-air missiles. (USN via LT J. Mizerak)

Chin Electronics Pods

F-14As carried a variety of under nose chin pods. Some contained ECM equipment, others contained infrared seekers, while still others contained television cameras or various combinations of equipment. Regardless of the chin pod carried, these aircraft were all F-14As.

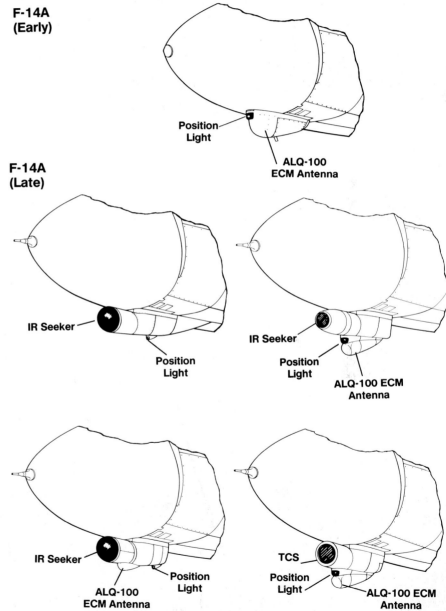

F-14A (Early)

Position Light

ALQ-100 ECM Antenna

F-14A (Late)

IR Seeker

Position Light

IR Seeker

Position Light

ALQ-100 ECM Antenna

IR Seeker

ALQ-100 ECM Antenna

Position Light

TCS

Position Light

ALQ-100 ECM Antenna

Retractable Refueling Probe

All F-14 Variants
(Starboard Side)

Refueling Probe Bay Door

Nozzle Assembly

Retracting Gear

An A-7E Corsair II of VA-146 refuels an F-14A of VF-211 over the Indian Ocean using a buddy store air-to-air refueling pod. Both aircraft are assigned to Carrier Air Wing 9 (CVW-9) aboard USS CONSTELLATION (CV-64) during May of 1980. The buddy refueling system consists of a fuel tank with an air driven pump, hose and drogue basket. (USN)

An Air Force KC-10A Extender refuels an F-14A of VF-211 Fighting Checkmates over the Arizona mountains during 1986. VF-211 was engaged in photographing other squadron aircraft that had been painted in various experimental water based camouflage paints. (LT Butch Kissick)

An F-14A of VF-211 takes on fuel from a KA-6D Intruder tanker over Arizona. The Tomcats are painted in water soluble experimental camouflage paints consisting of combinations of Dark, Medium and Light Grays and Light, Medium and Dark Browns. The paints took about four hours to apply and ten to remove. (LT Butch Kissick)

An F-14A of VF-21 Freelancers launches an AIM-54 Phoenix air-to-air missile during a live fire exercise. The Tomcat is equipped with a TCS chin pod and two 270 gallon fuel tanks. VF-21 was attached to Carrier Air Wing Fourteen (CVW-14) aboard USS CONSTELLATION (CV-64). (Hughes Aircraft)

An AN/ALE-39 Chaff-Flare dispenser is fitted on the port side of the tail hook on this F-14A (BuNo 160919) of VF-32 Swordsmen. The dispensers have a capacity of thirty chaff, flare or jammer cartridges. Chaff cartridges are filled with thin strips of wire that are equal in length to the wavelength of the hostile radar emitters. (Grumman via Hughes)

Ordnancemen load an AIM-7M Sparrow onto the port fuselage weapons bay on this F-14A. This version of the Sparrow was credited with shooting down one of the two MiG-23 Floggers credited to VF-32 Swordsmen on 5 January 1989. The AIM-7M has an improved monopulse seeker and digital processor giving it a greater look-down capability. (General Dynamics)

Red shirted Ordnancemen of VF-1 Wolfpack load an AIM-9D Sidewinder on the starboard wing rail of an F-14A aboard USS JOHN F. KENNEDY (CV-67) while another AIM-9D sits on the weapons dolly. The deck crew all have the Wolfpack insignia on their head/ear protection equipment known to the crews as the brain box. (USN by M. Langway)

An F-14A of VF-11 Red Rippers flies over the fjords of Norway during a NATO cruise aboard USS FORRESTAL (CV-59) during 1987. The Rippers were attached to Carrier Air Wing Six (CVW-6). This F-14A (BuNo 161871) was reconfigured to F-14A (Plus) standards during 1989. (USN)

F-14 Weapons

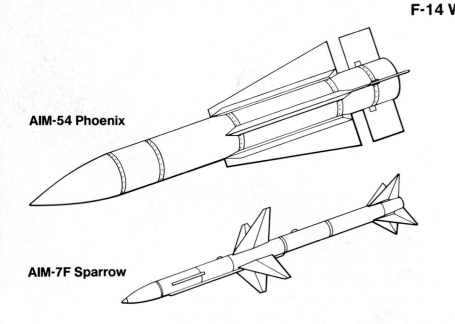

AIM-54 Phoenix

AIM-7F Sparrow

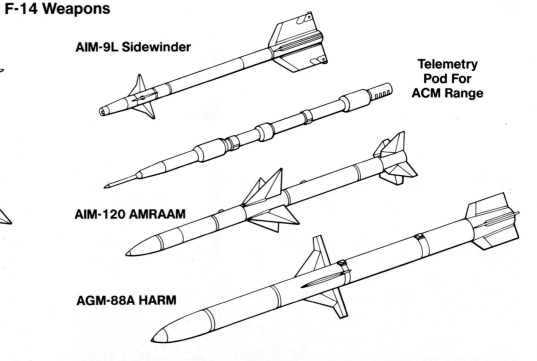

AIM-9L Sidewinder

Telemetry Pod For ACM Range

AIM-120 AMRAAM

AGM-88A HARM

M61-A1 Vulcan Cannon

All F-14 Variants

The M61-A1 Vulcan 20MM cannon has a normal rate of fire of 6,000 rounds per minute at a muzzle velocity of 3,400 feet per minute. The ammunition drum contains 675 rounds of 20MM ammunition which is fed to the gun via a flexible chute.

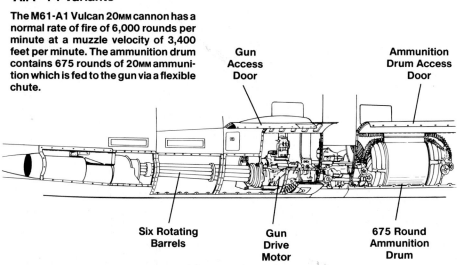

Gun Access Door

Ammunition Drum Access Door

Six Rotating Barrels

Gun Drive Motor

675 Round Ammunition Drum

The M61-A1 Vulcan cannon installation on the F-14A had a series of vents in the fuselage side behind the gun that allowed gun gases to escape. This prevented a buildup of these potentially explosive gases. The self-contained boarding ladder behind the gun is built in three sections which fold up into the fuselage. (Grumman)

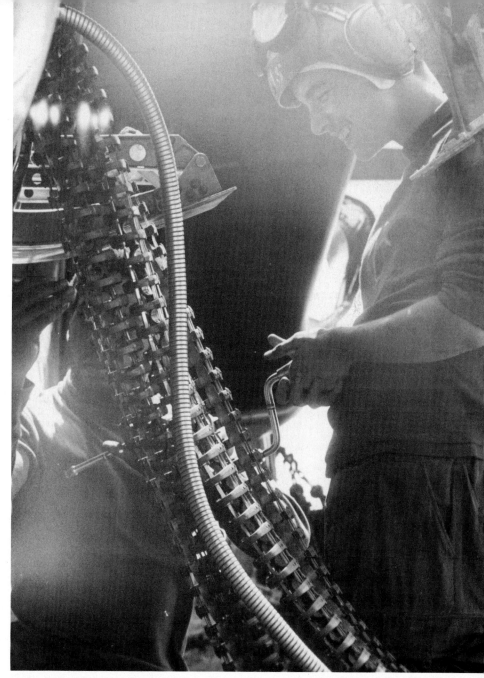

A Red shirted ordnanceman reloads the ammunition drum on an F-14A aboard USS CONSTELLATION (CV-64) during 1978. The ammunition drum has a capacity of 675 rounds. The General Electric M61-A1 Vulcan rotary cannon has a rate of fire in excess of 6,000 rounds per minute and is electrically driven. (USN)

This F-14A of VF-143 Pukin' Dogs is armed with an AIM-54 Phoenix missile on the forward pallet, an AIM-9 Sidewinder on the starboard wing pylon and an AIM-7 Sparrow on the port pylon. VF-143 was stationed aboard USS DWIGHT D. EISENHOWER (CVN-69) as part of Carrier Air Wing Seven (CVW-7). (USN)

This F-14A (BuNo 162692) of VF-143 Pukin' Dogs, flying over the Mediterranean Sea during April of 1988, is assigned to the squadron commander (as revealed by the side number 100 and full color markings). The squadron was assigned to CVW-7 aboard USS DWIGHT D. EISENHOWER (CVN-69). The Pukin' Dog and NAVY are Black, while the tail and fuselage stripes are Blue and White. (USN via LCDR Leen Houts)

An F-14A of VF-2 Bounty Hunters over the USS RANGER (CV-61) during 1988. The aircraft is overall Light Gull Gray with Red, White and Blue fuselage stripes. The rudders and ventral fins are Blue with Yellow stars. The underfuselage fuel tanks have a capacity of 270 gallons and the aircraft is fitted with a TCS chin pod. (Hughes Aircraft)

AN/ALE-39 Chaff/Flare Dispensers

Normally, only one dispenser is fitted although both can be carried if needed.

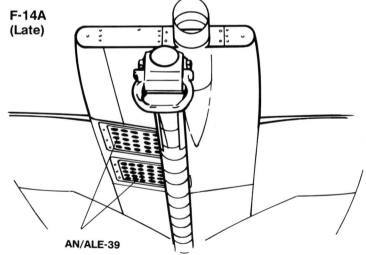

F-14A (Late)

AN/ALE-39

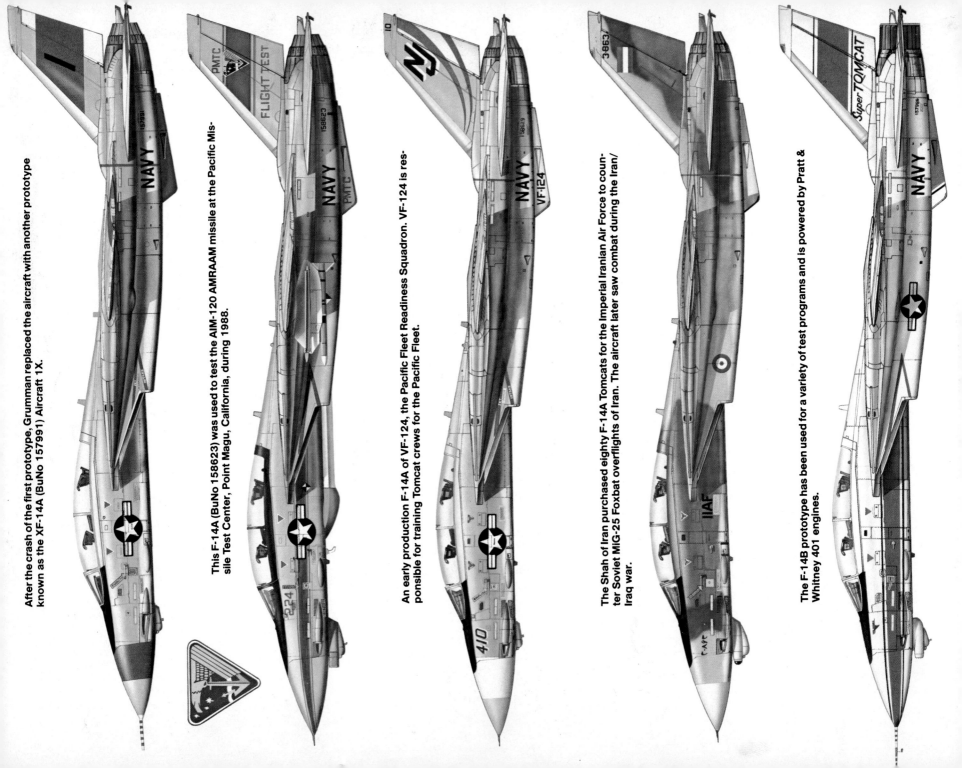

After the crash of the first prototype, Grumman replaced the aircraft with another prototype known as the XF-14A (BuNo 157991) Aircraft 1X.

This F-14A (BuNo 158623) was used to test the AIM-120 AMRAAM missile at the Pacific Missile Test Center, Point Magu, California, during 1988.

An early production F-14A of VF-124, the Pacific Fleet Readiness Squadron. VF-124 is responsible for training Tomcat crews for the Pacific Fleet.

The Shah of Iran purchased eighty F-14A Tomcats for the Imperial Iranian Air Force to counter Soviet MiG-25 Foxbat overflights of Iran. The aircraft later saw combat during the Iran/Iraq war.

The F-14B prototype has been used for a variety of test programs and is powered by Pratt & Whitney 401 engines.

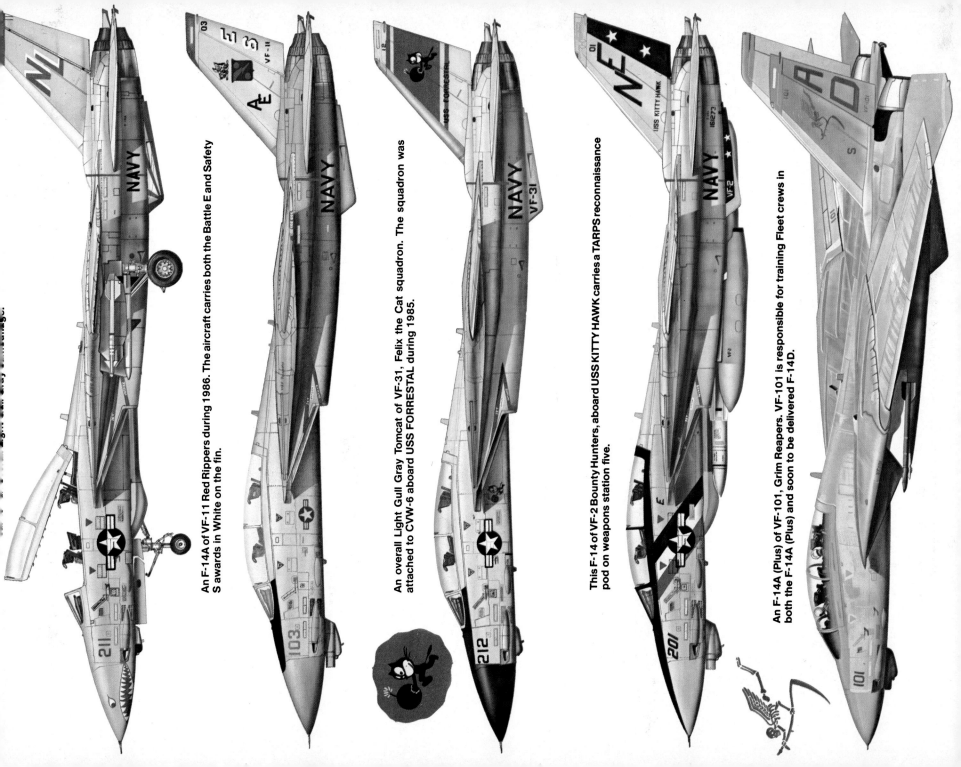

An F-14A of VF-11 Red Rippers during 1986. The aircraft carries both the Battle E and Safety S awards in White on the fin.

An overall Light Gull Gray Tomcat of VF-31, Felix the Cat squadron. The squadron was attached to CVW-6 aboard USS FORRESTAL during 1985.

This F-14 of VF-2 Bounty Hunters, aboard USS KITTY HAWK carries a TARPS reconnaissance pod on weapons station five.

An F-14A (Plus) of VF-101, Grim Reapers. VF-101 is responsible for training Fleet crews in both the F-14A (Plus) and soon to be delivered F-14D.

An early prototype of the Tactical Aerial Reconnaissance Pod System (TARPS) is mounted on the starboard engine nacelle during tests of the system held in 1973. This pod had horizontal fins at the rear of the pod and was mounted on the F-14's fuel tank hard point. (Grumman)

By 1980, the shape of the TARPS pod had evolved and the fins were removed. The fins were removed to make the pod closer in aerodynamic properties to the normal external fuel tanks carried by the Tomcat. The Black stripes on the TARPS pod are alignment reference markings. (Grumman)

The first of forty-seven F-14As built as dedicated TARPS aircraft was BuNo 160696. The production variant of the TARPS pod is now carried on the number 5 weapons station, leaving the fuselage hard points clear for fuel tanks. The pod is seventeen feet long and contains two cameras and an infrared line scanner. (Grumman)

TARPS equipped aircraft made their first cruise aboard USS NIMITZ (CVN-68) with VF-84 Jolly Rogers during 1982. When carrying a TARPS pod, the Tomcat can still carry other weapons for self defense. The pod utilizes cooling from the mother aircraft, similar to the system utilized by the AIM-54 Phoenix. (Grumman)

An F-14A of VF-51 positioned on the waist catapult of USS CARL VINSON in preparation for launch. Including catapult officers, it requires over thirty officers and deck crewmen to successfully launch an aircraft from the deck of an aircraft carrier. From plane handlers to ordnancemen, every job is important for safe operations. (USN by E. E. Cordero)

An F-14A of VF-24 Fighting Renegades launches from the waist catapult of USS KITTY HAWK (CV-63) during February of 1987. While the F-14A requires the use of afterburner during launch, the newer, re-engined F-14A (Plus) and F-14D do not. Currently, the KITTY HAWK is scheduled to replace the USS LEXINGTON (AVT-16) as the Navy's training carrier. (USN by J.D. Bunting)

Deck crews stand clear as an F-14A of VF-111 Sundowners is launched from the port catapult of USS CARL VINSON (CVN-70) during June of 1986. The Tomcat is armed with AIM-7 Sparrow air-to-air missiles and has a TCS pod under the nose. (USN via C. R. Solseth)

Vandy One, an overall Black F-14 of VX-4, flown by CDR Rich Fessendon, Squadron Exec and LT Jim Scholl (RIO), makes its last flight in this unusual color scheme during 1987. The Black scheme and Playboy Bunny character had also been carried earlier on three F-4 Phantoms of VX-4. (McDonnell-Douglas by Harry Gann)

COMBAT

American relations with Libya were peaceful until COL Moammar El Gadhafi overthrew King Idris I. Once firmly in power, COL Gadhafi began a campaign of hate and terrorism against the West and, in particular, the U.S. He felt that the West had taken advantage of the Libyan people to gain access to their oil reserves. As part of his expansionist plans, Gadhafi declared that the territorial limit of Libyan waters extended out twelve miles. The U.S. felt this claim to be unlawful and set into motion a challenge to the Libyan leader.

The first shooting incident took place on 19 August 1981 in the Gulf of Sidra. Although the Libyans had fired on Navy aircraft that violated the twelve mile limit, the Navy had not returned the fire, since no Navy aircraft had been hit. Early in the morning on 19 August, two Libyan Sukhoi Su-22 Fitters took off from the former Wheelus Air Force Base near Tripoli and were vectored by coastal radar toward two patrolling F-14A Tomcats. The two F-14s of VF-41, call signs Fast Eagle 102 (flown by CDR Harry "Hank" Kleeman with LT David Venlet as his Radar Intercept Officer) and Fast Eagle 107 (LT Larry "Music" Muczynski and RIO LTJG Jim "Amos" Anderson), were flying CAP for the USS NIMITZ (CVN-68) battle group while other aircraft were conducting a missile firing exercise. A patrolling E-2A Hawkeye made radar contact on the two Su-22s coming directly toward the F-14s at a high rate of speed and reported their presence. The Fitters were flying in close formation while the Tomcats were over one mile apart flying in a loose combat spread formation. The combat spread formation gave the Tomcats the advantage, allowing them greater flexibility in maneuvering at transonic or high subsonic speeds.

As the Libyan fighters closed on the Tomcats, the lead Fitter fired an AA-2 Atoll air-to-air missile, which failed to guide at the Navy jets. The two Su-22s were immediately declared hostile, and the Tomcats were cleared to engage. The F-14s executed an offensive split with CDR Kleeman going high after the Libyan wingman and LT Muczynski going low after the leader. When the Libyan wingman turned clear of the sun, CDR Kleeman fired a single AIM-9L Sidewinder. The Sidewinder guided, flew up the tailpipe of the Fitter and exploded. The Lybian pilot successfully ejected from his burning Su-22.

LT Muczynski fired on his target at extremely close range and when the AIM-9L exploded, debris from the Fitter filled the sky. LT Muczynski had to break hard to avoid flying into the debris and possibly damaging his aircraft. In the world's first engagement between swing wing aircraft, the F-14 had proven both its superiority and the superiority of U.S. Navy crews.

Four years later, F-14s of the 6th Fleet were involved in another encounter over the Mediterranean. On 7 October 1985, the Italian cruise liner ACHILLE LAURO was hijacked by Palestine Liberation Organization (PLO) terrorists under the command of Mohammed Abbas as it left the Port of Alexandria, Egypt. The hijacking was an attempt to pressure the Israeli government to release political prisoners, including a number of known terrorists. The Egyptian government promised safe passage to Italy if Abbas would let the kidnapped passengers go free. Unknown to the Egyptian government, Abbas or one of his henchmen had already killed an American passenger, Leon Klinghoffer. Accepting the Egyptian offer, Abbas and the hijackers escaped to Syria, then to Egypt where they boarded an Egypt Air Boeing 737.

U.S. intelligence had uncovered that Abbas and his group were on the 737 and President Regan ordered the Sixth Fleet to take action. The plan was to intercept the Egypt Air flight and direct it to land at a friendly base where the terrorists could be taken into custody. The 737 was located by an E-2C Hawkeye and a flight of four F-14s of Fighting

AJ-102 (Fast Eagle 102), an F-14A of VF-41 Black Aces, was one of the two F-14As that engaged and shot down two Libyan Sukhoi Su-22 Fitters over the Gulf of Sidra. AJ-102 was flown by CDR Harry Kleeman with LT David Venlet serving as his RIO. (USN by Phil D. Tesner)

Squadron Seventy Four (VF-74), off USS SARATOGA (CV-60), was vectored for the intercept. Approaching the 737 with all lighting extinguished, the F-14s took up position on either wing, ahead and to the rear. A call was made to the pilot of the 737 to follow, and he had no choice but to obey. The F-14s escorted the 737 to Sigonella Military Base near Catania, Sicily. A small victory in the long war against terrorism.

The second air-to-air combat and third major incident over the Mediterranean again involved the Libyans. On 4 January 1989 two F-14As of VF-32, AC-202 and AC-207, were on Combat Air Patrol off USS JOHN F. KENNEDY (CV-67) when two MiG-23 Floggers, that had taken off from Al Bumbaw Airfield, Tobruk, began closing on the Tomcats. The MiGs began maneuvering for an engagement against the two F-14s, which were about 50 miles off of the Libyan coast. During the eight minute engagement the MiGs kept turning into the F-14s to maintain a firing solution for their AA-7 Apex missiles. After a number of maneuvers designed to open the distance and evade the Libyans, it was decided that the MiGs had hostile intent and the F-14s were cleared to engage.

The lead F-14, AC 202, was flown by the Squadron commanding officer and launched an AIM-7 Sparrow missile, which missed. With the MiGs closing, the wingman, flying in AC 207, also launched a Sparrow, which tracked and destroyed one MiG. The Libyan pilot successfully ejected and a good chute was observed. The F-14 leader closed to within range for an AIM-9 Sidewider and maneuvered into a firing position. The Sidewinder guided on the tailpipe of the MiG-23 and hit the aircraft in the rear fuselage. The Libyan pilot was able to eject from his crippled MiG before it hit the water. The F-14 leader radioed the Combat Information Center (CIC) aboard the JFK, *Roger, two Floggers. Two Floggers splashed. We're heading north.*

In three aerial encounters, the F-14 has emerged the victor and has proven its worth in combat over the hostile environment of the Mediterranean Sea.

This F-14A had the call sign Fast Eagle 102 and was flown by CDR Hank Kleeman of VF-41 Black Aces off USS NIMITZ (CVN-68) during the Gulf of Sidra incident. Fast Eagle 102 (along with Fast Eagle 107) was responsible for downing two Libyan Su-22 Fitters on 19 August 1981. (USN by J. Brown)

The four Naval aviators of VF-41 that were involved in the 19 August 1981 Gulf of Sidra incident pose in front of the second F-14 involved in the shoot down, Fast Eagle 107. They are (left to right): LTJG James (Amos) Anderson, LT Larry (Music) Muczynski, CDR Hank Kleeman (CO of VF-41) and LT Dave Venlet. Both Fitters were shot down using AIM-9L Sidewinders. (USN by Phil D. Tesner)

A Libyan Su-22 Fitter H on patrol over the Mediterranean Sea on 18 August 1981. This Su-22 is carrying two AA-2 (K-13A) ATOLL IR guided air-to-air missiles and two external fuel tanks, the same configuration as on the two Fitters involved in the 19 August incident. Libya was the only export customer for this variant of the Fitter. (USN)

A pair of Libyan flown MiG-23 Floggers over the Mediterranean near the coast of Libya. Unlike these Floggers, the MiG-23s engaged by the VF-32 Tomcats were armed with AA-7 Apex and AA-8 Aphid air-to-air missiles. The MiG's armament was confirmed by use of the TCS system on one of the Tomcats. (via Nicholas J. Waters III)

Purple shirted fuel crew refuel a Sidewinder armed F-14 of VF-74 Bedevilers prior to a mission over the Mediterranean Sea during 1986. Four aircraft of VF-74, flying off USS SARATOGA (CV-60), intercepted the Egypt Air Boeing 737 that was carrying the hijackers of the ACHILLE LAURO on 11 October 1986. (USN by W. A. Shayka)

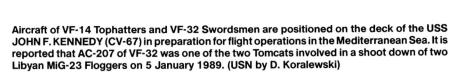

Aircraft of VF-14 Tophatters and VF-32 Swordsmen are positioned on the deck of the USS JOHN F. KENNEDY (CV-67) in preparation for flight operations in the Mediterranean Sea. It is reported that AC-207 of VF-32 was one of the two Tomcats involved in a shoot down of two Libyan MiG-23 Floggers on 5 January 1989. (USN by D. Koralewski)

This F-14A of VF-32 Swordsmen (AC-207) was reported to be one of the two aircraft involved in the downing of two Libyan MiG-23 Floggers over the Mediterranean Sea on 5 January 1989. The Tomcat carries the latest tactical camouflage and has the squadron's sword marking painted on the fuel tank and Swordsmen painted on the wing glove leading edge. (David F. Brown)

Iranian F-14A Program

During 1974, the Shah of Iran, Mohammed Riza Sha Pahlevi, contracted with Grumman (through the Foreign Military Assistance Command) for thirty Grumman F-14A Tomcats for the Imperial Iranian Air Force (NIROU HAYAI SHAH AHAN SHAHAHIYE IRAN). The Shah wanted the Tomcats to counter the overflights of Iran by Soviet MiG-25 Foxbats. The Soviets had been making regular Foxbat flights over the north-eastern border region and the IIAF had nothing capable of intercepting the high flying reconnaissance aircraft. During 1975, a second batch of fifty F-14As was ordered. The aircraft, produced between Block 90 and Block 95, were assigned Navy BuNos 160299 through 160378, for accounting purposes.

Externally, Iranian F-14As were identical to the F-14As being flown by the U.S. Navy, with the exception of the refueling probe bay door, which was deleted. Internally, the IIAF F-14s differed in the capabilities of the AWG-9 fire control system, the electronic counter measure (ECM) systems installed and the AIM-54 missiles. All of the electronic and missile systems were greatly downgraded, since it was felt that if any of the sophisticated electronic system were to fall into unfriendly hands it would put the U.S. at a disadvantage. This theory turned into fact when a disgruntled Iranian Air Force pilot flew an F-14A across the Soviet border during the Iran/Iraq War and landed at a Soviet military airfield. The pilot and aircraft were impounded and neither have been heard from since.

Deliveries of F-14As to the IIAF began during January of 1976 and all but one aircraft had been delivered by July of 1978. Iran had also ordered 424 AIM-54A Phoenix missiles, but by 1979 only 270 had been delivered. The Tomcats were assigned to four squadrons stationed at Khatami Air Base near Isfahan and at Shiraz Air Bases. Both these bases were located near the Iran/Soviet border.

During 1977, the Shah had expressed an interest in purchasing an additional seventy F-14s, with an estimated value of 900 million dollars. This sale was never consummated since Grumman was engaged in producing the initial Iranian order and the political climate in Iran had become extremely unstable. Between 1976 and February of 1979 the IIAF lost three F-14As to various accidents. On 16 January 1979, the Shah of Iran was deposed by the dissident Ayatollah Khomeini. Shortly after the fall of the Shah, supplies of spare parts to keep the F-14s operational were stopped and the Grumman technicians were called home. The newly renamed Islamic Republic of Iran Air Force (IRIAF) was forced to maintain the F-14s with their own technicians and with foreign technicians hired from various western and asian nations.

In September of 1980, the Iran-Iraq war broke out when neither side could agree to a 1975 treaty that gave Iran control of the oil rich territory of Khuzistan. During the war, Iran was able to keep anywhere from seven to ten F-14As operational at any one time (although Iranian claims are much higher). By 1986, there were no Phoenix missiles operational and the aircraft were armed with Sidewinder and Sparrow missiles. Throughout the war a severe shortage of tires and brakes kept the majority of F-14s grounded and an effort to locally produce tires and brake pads proved fruitless. The Iranians had to rely on the unreliable aircraft parts black market, which managed to keep a small amount of spares coming into the country.

During the Iran-Iraq war the Iranians lost at least three F-14s in air-to-air combat. Two were shot down by Mirage F-1 fighters and one was shot down by a MiG-21, reportedly armed with French Matra Magic air-to-air missiles. The Iranians normally used

F-14As on the ramp at Shivaz Air Base, Iran, prepare to start engines for a training mission during 1977. These aircraft are from the second production batch of fifty aircraft ordered during 1975. The IIAF Tomcats had the door covering the refueling probe bay deleted. (Grumman)

The Shah of Iran ordered a total of eighty F-14As to be delivered between 1975 and 1978. The order consisted of two separate production batches of thirty and fifty aircraft each. Production of the Iranian Air Force aircraft took place alongside F-14As for the Navy. (Grumman)

An F-14 of the Imperial Iranian Air Force parked on the ramp at the Grumman plant at Calverton, New York, awaiting a flight crew to make the delivery flight to Iran. Aircraft was finished in a Tan, Brown and Green uppersurface camouflage over a Light Gray undersurface. (Grumman)

the F-14 in a radar warning role, using the aircraft's AWG-9 system. These F-14s flew singly (sometimes backed up by F-4Es and/or F-5Es). This left the Tomcat at a disadvantage compared to the normal air-to-air combat tactics that called for a flight of two: leader and wingman.

The IRIAF claimed that F-14As destroyed one Iraqi Mirage F-1 and two MiG-21s. The IRIAF kill ratio would have been much better if they had been able to employ the Tomcat in the fighter role with proper fighter tactics and had been able to maintain the Phoenix missile systems. The inadequate maintenance and lack of spare parts kept the F-14 fleet restricted to such low numbers that they were never really able to take an active

part in the air war.

The F-14As in IRIAF service were camouflaged in a Tan, Brown and Green uppersurface patter over a Light Gray undersurfaces. The Iranian insignia was a Green, White and Red roundel carried in four positions (as per U.S. practice) and a Green, White, Red fin flash on the vertical fins. The IIAF gave the initial Block of thirty F-14As serial numbers 3-863 through 3-893. The second Block of fifty carried serials 3-6001 thru 3-6051. Deliveries were made by air, being flown from Bethpage, N.Y. (in temporary U.S. markings) to Iran. The U.S. national insignia was replaced by Iranian roundels once the aircraft were in Iran.

An F-14A (IIAF serial 3-863) on an acceptance flight during 1975. The Iranian F-14s had the sensitive AWG-9 radar/fire control system, computer software, AIM-54A missiles and electronic counter measures systems greatly degraded. This security measure proved wise, since at least one IIAF Tomcat ended up in unfriendly hands. (Grumman)

A flight of IIAF F-14s near Mach 1 (wing vanes extended) as they approach the Elbruz Mountains north of Tehran, Iran. When committed to combat during the Iran-Iraq war, the IIAF F-14As operated singly. This tactic resulted in the loss of at least three F-14As in air-to-air combat. (Grumman)

This Iranian F-14A (serial number 3-6046) was one of the last purchased by Iran. The aircraft carries pallets for Phoenix missiles on fuselage as well as wing missile pylons. During the Iran-Iraq war the aircraft were mainly flown armed with AIM-7 Sparrow and AIM-9 Sidewinder missiles. (Grumman)

Iranian Air Force F-14As retained all of the aircraft's carrier equipment, such as catapult launch bar and arresting hook, although the hook was now used for airfield arresting gear. Iran purchased the F-14A to counter overflights by Soviet MiG-25 Foxbats. The leading edges of the wings, horizontal stabilizers and vertical stabilizers were unpainted. (Grumman)

For delivery to Iran, the Tomcats carried temporary U.S. national insignia over the Iranian roundels. These Tomcats are new production aircraft waiting to be delivered to the IIAF and U.S. Navy. The IIAF F-14s were flown to Iran via Europe. (Grumman)

Refueling Probe Bay Door

USN
F-14A

IIAF
F-14A

Door
Deleted

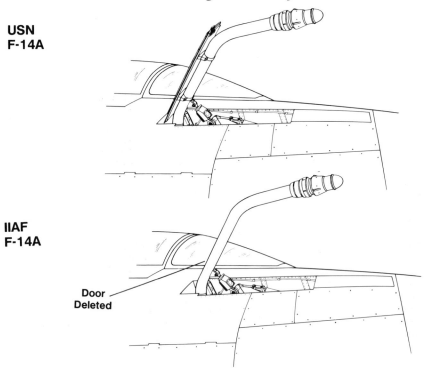

F-14B

The F-14B resulted from a Navy/Grumman program aimed at replacing the troublesome TF-30 engines of the F-14A with more reliable and powerful Pratt & Whitney F-401-P400 engines. Two F-14A airframes (BuNo 157986 and BuNo 158630) were converted to serve as prototype aircraft for the F-14B Super Tomcat program. The first prototype, BuNo 157986, was fitted with two 28,100 lbst Pratt and Whitney F-401-P400 turbofan engines replacing the 20,900 lbst Pratt and Whitney TF-30-412A engines. Besides the increase in thrust, the new engines had another advantage; they weighed some 600 pounds less. Additionally, the F-401-P400 was a derivative of the Pratt and Whitney F100-PW-100 engine, used in the McDonnell Douglas F-15A Eagle and had a degree of commonality with the Air Force power plant. The first F-14B prototype made its first flight on 12 September 1973 and, after completion of a series of flight tests, the aircraft was withdrawn from service and placed into long term storage.

During 1981, the F-14B prototype (BuNo 157986) was taken out of storage and fitted with a pair of General Electric F101DFE (Derivative Fighter Engines). After a short initial flight test program, the F-14B was put through an evaluation program that lasted thirty-three flight hours. Beginning on 14 July 1981, some twenty-two Grumman and three Navy test flights were conducted with the F-14B which revealed a number of technical problems with the engine installation. Grumman, however, discovered that with the F101DFE engines, the F-14B could accelerate from Mach 0.8 to Mach 1.8 in ninety seconds. The F-14B was also able to be catapulted from a carrier deck without the use of the afterburner. Navy test pilots found out that with the additional thrust, they were able to fly the aircraft, rather than the engines, as they had to do in the standard F-14A.

At a normal combat weight of 65,000 pounds, the F-101DFE powered F-14B had a power to weight ratio of almost one to one. This enabled the F-14B to accelerate while in the vertical, a maneuver the standard TF-30 powered F-14A could not accomplish.

Externally, the F-14B appeared identical to the F-14A except for the engines and the addition of a television camera system test pod. The aircraft carried no AWG-9 radar system, the space being taken up by the racks for specialized test instruments. The test program was terminated in September of 1981 and again the F-14B prototype was placed in storage.

A second F-14B (BuNo 158630) was being built when, in September of 1981, the Navy cancelled the F-14B program and decided that it would continue F-14A production with the Pratt and Whitney TF30-412A engines. As a result, the second prototype (BuNo 158630) was converted back to a late production F-14A.

In July of 1984, a contract was issued to Grumman to install General Electric augmented turbofan F110-GE-400 engines in the F-14B prototype and in July of 1986, initial flight testing began. The tests proved highly successful and led directly to the Navy decision to go ahead with the F-14A (PLUS).

During 1988, a joint contract was issued to Martin-Marietta and General Electric to develop a dual chin optical/electronics pod for the Tomcat that would contain both the Television Camera Set (TCS) and the Infrared Search and Track Set (IRSTS). This dual pod was successfully test flown on the F-14B prototype and is programed to become part of the F-14D program.

The F-14B prototype has been used to test the various upgrades that are to be used on late production F-14s. When the aircraft is not needed for testing, it is placed in temporary or long term storage at Bethpage until needed.

F-14C

At one point during the F-14B program, Grumman proposed an updated development of the F-14B to be designated the F-14C. The F-14C was to have incorporated upgraded avionics, an improved radar and a fire control system compatible with the E-2C, A-6E and FA-18. It was to have been powered by the General Electric F-101DFE (Derivative Fighter Engines) turbofan engines being tested on the F-14B. Other proposed features included a programmable signal processor, increased computer memory, Honeywell laser-gyro Inertial Navigation System, a non-cooperative target identification system and a television camera system (TCS). All of these features were later incorporated into late production F-14As, the F-14A (Plus) and some are programed for the F-14D. In the event, the Navy decided not to produce the F-14C aircraft.

Tomcat 21

Another proposal, made by Grumman to meet the requirements of the Advanced Tactical Fighter (ATF) program, used the company designation Tomcat 21. The Tomcat 21 proposal, if accepted, would result in an aircraft more advanced than the F-14D. The Tomcat 21 would feature an airframe made up of more composite materials to reduce the aircraft's considerable radar signature and the addition of avionics that would allow the Tomcat 21 to attack ground targets, while retaining its air-to-air capability. The Tomcat 21 would be powered by high bypass turbofan engines to increase fuel efficiency (and range).

At the present time, Grumman has not received the funding necessary to proceed with research and development ($2 billion) and prototype construction. If funding should be forthcoming, the Tomcat 21 program would result in an aircraft with ninety percent of the required capability of the Advanced Tactical Fighter (ATF) for about sixty percent of the cost of a totally new aircraft.

The number seven F-14A prototype on the ramp at Grumman just before being re-engined with Pratt and Whitney F-401-PW400 turbofans. With the new engines, the Navy designated the aircraft the F-14B and Grumman named it the Super Tomcat. The aircraft was in overall Gloss Insignia White with Red stripes and Black trim. (Grumman)

The F-14B prototype (BuNo 157986) differed externally from the F-14A in the shape of the engine exhaust nozzles of the Pratt and Whitney F-401 turbofans. The F-14B prototype would later serve in the development programs for both the F-14A (Plus) and F-14D. (Grumman)

During 1981 the F-14B was removed from storage and fitted with General Electric F-101-GE-400 Derivative Fighter Engines (DFE). During the short flight test program (between July and September 1981) Grumman made twenty-two flights and the Navy conducted three test flights. The aircraft carried a General Electric logo on the ventral fin. (Grumman)

The first F-14B (BuNo 157986) taxies out for its first flight from Calverton, New York on 12 September 1973. The F-14B did not carry the AWG-9 radar system, using the space for special test equipment. A Tomcat insignia has been placed on the tail. (Grumman)

The F-14B (BuNo 157986) prototype with the General Electric Derivative Fighter Engines (DFE) made its first flight on 14 July 1981. The DFE engines were modular in design to ease production and maintenance. Because of these tests, GE engines were selected to power the F-14A (Plus) and the F-14D. (Grumman)

During 1988, the F-14B prototype aircraft was used to test a General Electric/Martin Marietta designed dual electro/optical chin pod that contained both a Television Camera System (TCS) and an Infrared Search and Track Set (IRSTS). The TCS/IRSTS pod was successful and was selected for installation on the F-14D. (Grumman)

The F-14B prototype, in formation with a Northrop F-5 of VF-43, flies over the Atlantic during 1981. The General Electric F101 DFE engines provided the F-14B with considerably more thrust than the standard Pratt and Whitney TF-30-P412 engines. The GE F101 engine was originally designed for the Rockwell B-1 and was also tested in the General Dynamics F-16. (Grumman)

The F-14B Super Tomcat on the ramp at the Grumman facility during 1976. The natural metal APU (Auxiliary Power Unit) exhaust area is visible just forward of NAVY on the lower fuselage side. Once flight testing with the F-401 engine was completed, the F-14B was put into long term storage. (Grumman)

The F-14B test aircraft is fitted with General Electric F110-GE-400 engines and a dual infrared sensor/ECM chin pod under the nose. Although the aircraft was used as a testbed, it retained the M61 cannon. All leading edge surfaces were unpainted natural metal. (Grumman)

The F-14B prototype carries Phoenix missiles on the fuselage pallets, Sparrows on the wing pylons, and Sidewinders on the wing shoulder pylons during early 1987. The aircraft was also equipped with two 270 gallon fuel tanks. Even though it is carrying Phoenix missiles, the aircraft could not fire them, since it had no AWG-9 radar installed. (Grumman)

The F-14B program originally had two aircraft assigned. The second aircraft was BuNo 158630 and when the F-14B program was canceled during 1971, the aircraft was reconfigured to F-14A standards. The aircraft was issued to VF-201, Carrier Air Reserve Wing Twenty (CVWR-20) at NAS Dallas, Texas. (Grumman)

F-14A (Plus)

In July of 1984, the Navy issued Grumman an 863.8 million dollar fixed price contract covering a Full Scale Development (FSD) program aimed at upgrading the F-14A. General Electric (engines) and Hughes (fire control system) were named as program sub-contractors. The F-14A FSD program included upgrades to the F-14A's avionics, airborne intercept radar and most importantly the installation of improved and more powerful engines. One of the major problems the Navy had identified with the F-14A had been the unreliability of the TF-30 engines.

The FSD program specifically identified the General Electric F-110-GE-400 engine as the replacement for the Pratt & Whitney TF30. Additionally, a Fatigue/Engine Monitoring System (FEMS), an ARC-182 UHF/VHF radio installation, a Direct Lift Control/Approach Power Control (DLC/AFC MOD), an ALR-67 Threat Warning and Recognition System, an AWG-15F Hughes Radar Fire Control System and a gun gas purge system were all specified to be part of the upgrade program.

Under the Naval Air Systems Command (NAVAIRSYSCOM) contract (number N00019-84-C0015), the FSD aircraft would be built during fiscal year 1986, beginning with Fabrication Number 558 (BuNo 162910) and would be in block 145 configuration. Six aircraft were involved in the flight test development program (including the F-14B prototype BuNo 157986). The first flight of an F-14A (Plus) FSD aircraft (BuNo 162910) took place during September of 1986 from Grumman's Calverton Test Flight Center.

The F-14A (Plus) differs externally from a late production F-14A by the larger engine exhausts of the F-110 engine, the radar warning ECM antenna fairings mounted under the wing glove, a gun installation with a gun gas purge system and the deletion of the wing glove vanes.

The heart of the F-14A (Plus) is the power plant: two General Electric F-110-GE-400 augmented turbofan engines. The F-110-GE-400 is a hybrid engine, combining the proven core sections of the GE F-101 and F-110-GE-100 engines used in the General Dynamics F-16 and the McDonnell-Douglas F-15. The engine retains some eighty-two percent parts commonality with the F-101 and F-110-GE-100, greatly easing Department of Defense/Navy spare parts procurement. For production purposes and to enable the engine to be retrofitted into earlier production F-14As, a four foot two inch plug was inserted in the afterburner section. Other minor internal structural modifications were required to conform to the existing air inlet location.

The F-110-GE-400 has a rated power of 28,200 pounds of thrust (lbst) an increase of 7,300 lbst per engine. This increase in power enables the F-14A (Plus) to be catapult launched without the use of the afterburners. The General Electric engines also offer significant improvements in fuel economy, which gives the F-14A (Plus) some sixty percent more range, one third more time on station and a sixty-one percent improvement in rate of climb.

The F-110-GE-400 is a high bypass turbofan designed for modular assembly, which not only facilitates assembly and repair, but also eases routine maintenance. Borescope ports are positioned over numerous critical parts of the engine assembly such as the combusters, turbines and the compressor section. The F-110 allows unrestricted throttle movement throughout the aircraft's flight envelope with no stagnation stalls or visible smoke trails. The pilot's workload during landing, thanks to the increase in available thrust, has been greatly reduced, allowing the pilot to fly the aircraft rather than the engines.

Production of the F-14A (Plus) began in March of 1987 with the first aircraft being delivered to the Navy at the Naval Air Test Center, Patuxent River, Maryland, during

The first production F-14A (Plus) on the ramp at the Grumman facility. The aircraft was Fabrication Number 558 (BuNo 162910). The engine nozzles for the General Electric F110-GE-400 are larger than those of the TF-30s used on the standard F-14A. The aircraft was delivered to NATC, Patuxent River, Maryland during December of 1987 for acceptance tests by the Navy. (Grumman)

November. During early 1988, a number of F-14A (Plus) aircraft were sent to Point Mugu, California, to take part in missile development tests at the Pacific Missile Test Center (PMTC). These tests were flown by Test and Evaluation Squadron Four (VX-4). On 15 April 1988, an F-14A (Plus) began carrier suitability testing aboard USS INDEPENDENCE (CV-62) in the Pacific Ocean.

A total of thirty-eight F-14A (Plus) aircraft were produced in three separate blocks: eighteen aircraft (BuNo 162910 through 162927) in Block 145, fifteen aircraft (BuNo 163215 through 163229) in Block 150 and five aircraft (BuNo 163407 through 163411) in Block 155.

During early 1988, Fighter Squadron One Hundred and One (VF-101) became the first squadron to transition to the F-14A (Plus). Fighter Squadron Seventy-four (VF-74), the Bedevilers, under the command of CDR Gus Grissom, Jr., was the second squadron, transitioning to the F-14A (Plus) at Naval Air Station Oceana, Virginia, during early 1989. By April of 1989, the squadron had eight F-14A (Plus) aircraft on strength and by late 1989 they had received their full complement of ten. CDR Grissom, along with his RIO LTJG Bob McGee, were the first crew to launch an AIM-54A Phoenix from the F-14A (Plus). CDR Grissom stated, *"We have found the A (Plus) to be an exceptionally impressive aircraft in performance. At 5,000 feet it will accelerate from 200 knots to 600 knots in twenty-four seconds — it adds 50 knots every three seconds. The new Direct Lift Control (DLC) system makes the last second corrections in the landing pattern at the ship much easier to accomplish."*

XF-52 is an F-14A (Plus) of the Pacific Missile Test Center, Point Mugu, California. Weapons testing with the F-14A (Plus) began at PMTC during January of 1988. Tests included firing air-to-air missiles, carrying Mk-82 500 pound bombs, and both air-to-air and air-to-ground firing of the internal cannon. (General Electric)

The first East Coast Tomcat squadron to transition to the F-14A (Plus) was VF-101 Grim Reapers, the Atlantic Fleet Replacement Air Group (RAG). VF-101 received their first F-14A (Plus) during April of 1988. Besides the engine exhausts, the F-14A (Plus) differs from the F-14A in the gas gun purge system air intakes on the port side of the aircraft. (USN via Bill Ennis)

Engine Development

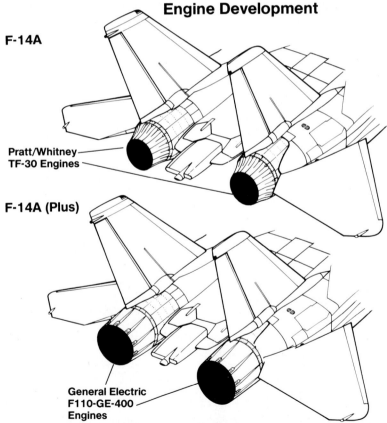

F-14A

Pratt/Whitney TF-30 Engines

F-14A (Plus)

General Electric F110-GE-400 Engines

An F-14A (Plus) of VF-101 on a practice mission high over the Atlantic during 1989. The squadron trains aircrews for Atlantic Fleet squadrons on the F-14A (Plus), preparing the pilots and RIOs for squadron assignments. (Grumman)

Wing Glove Vane

VF-74 Bedevilers became the first operational squadron to re-equip with the F-14A (Plus) during August of 1988. This squadron was responsible for the intercept of the Egypt Air 737 carrying the hijackers of the ACHILLE LAURO during 1985. (USN by LTJG Jack MacDonald)

F-14A

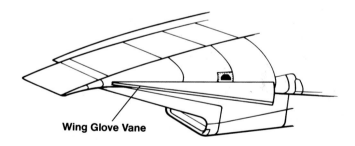

Wing Glove Vane

F-14A (Plus)

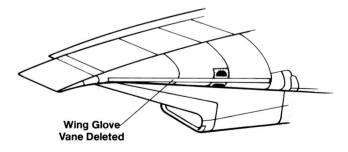

Wing Glove Vane Deleted

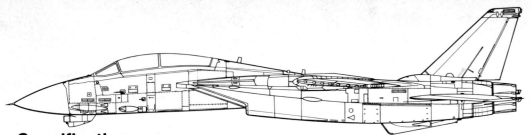

Specifications
Grumman F-14A (Plus) Tomcat

Wingspan	64 feet 1 ½ inches
Length	62 feet 8 inches
Height	16 feet
Empty Weight	41,780 pounds
Maximum Weight	74,349 pounds
Powerplant	Two General Electric 27,000 lbst F-110-GE-400 turbofan engines.
Armament	One M61-A1 20мм cannon (internal), six AIM-54C Phoenix or six AIM-7 Sparrow or six AIM-120 AMRAAM and two AIM-9 Sidewinder missiles.

Performance

Maximum Speed	1,544 mph
Service ceiling	53,000 feet
Range	2,000 miles (with tanks)
Crew	Two

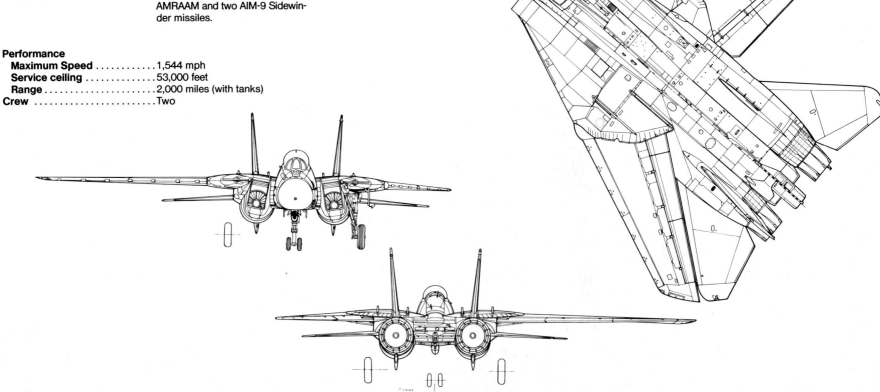

A VF-101 Grim Reapers F-14A (Plus) over the Virginia countryside near NAS Oceana during 1989. With the new General Electric engines, F-14A (Plus) can accelerate from 250 knots to 600 knots in just twenty seconds. (Grumman)

This F-14A (Plus) of VF-101 Grim Reapers is equipped with the Northrop developed Television Camera Set (TCS) pod under the nose. The aircraft is finished in overall Medium Gull Gray and carries an S (for Safety) on the vertical stabilizer. (USN via Bill Ennis)

Gun Gas Purge System

F-14A

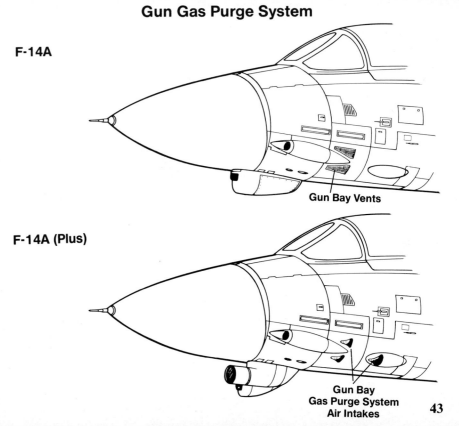

Gun Bay Vents

F-14A (Plus)

Gun Bay
Gas Purge System
Air Intakes

The F-14A (Plus) is the forerunner of the Super Tomcat F-14D. The F-14D will use the same engine/airframe of the F-14A (Plus) modified with upgraded electronics, radar, communications equipment and state-of-the-art cockpit displays. (Grumman)

An F-14A (Plus) flies over NAS Oceana, Virginia, the home base of VF-101 Grim Reapers. Pilots report that the F-14A (Plus) has a much better acceleration and can perform vertical maneuvers that were impossible in the TF-30 powered F-14A. The two fairings under the wing glove are ECM antennas. (Grumman)

Radar Warning ECM Fairings

F-14A

F-14A (Plus)

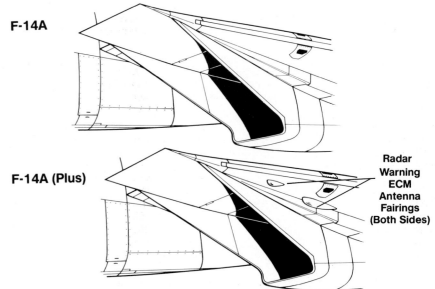

Radar Warning ECM Antenna Fairings (Both Sides)

NASA Tomcat

In June of 1985, the National Aeronautics and Space Administration's Ames-Dryden Flight Research Facility at Edwards Air Force Base, California, (in conjunction with the Navy and Grumman) began a series of experiments with a flight control system known as the Aileron-Rudder Interconnect or ARI. The system was installed on an F-14A Tomcat (aircraft number 1X, BuNo 157991) loaned to NASA by the Navy. The ARI was designed to coordinate turns, prevent wing rock and resist spins during conditions of high angle of attack.

In earlier high angle of attack flight tests with the F-14 conducted by Chuck Sewell, Grumman's chief test pilot, Chuck had noted that the F-14 experienced a loss of roll response. These tests totaled sixteen flights, during which Sewell was able to control the aircraft at high angles of attack, even though air speed dropped to somewhere between 0 and 30 knots. These tests were made with the aircraft in a clean configuration. The disadvantage in the loss of roll response at high angles of attack was that, in combat, an F-14A in a steep nose high climb would not be able to rapidly change direction by rolling into a turn.

For the ARI tests, extensive modifications were made to the aircraft's analog flight control system and the nose was modified with movable canard control surfaces. The flight control system modifications included a cross control feature that allowed the pilot to roll the aircraft opposite to lateral stick input, by use of rudder pedal input. This gave the F-14 pilot roll response for tactical maneuvering while the aircraft was at a high angle of attack (i.e. nose up climb).

The ARI tests were made by three Navy pilots and one Grumman test pilot. Two of the Navy pilots were from the Naval Air Test Center at Patuxent River, Maryland, while the third was from the Pacific Missile Test Center at Point Mugu, California.

The tests showed that the ARI modifications gave the Tomcat improved roll performance at high angles of attack (above 30 degrees), while retaining spin resistance and wing rock suppression. With the ARI system installed, the pilots reported that there was no reduction in the good basic flying qualities of the F-14. The tests were made in both a clean configuration and while carrying external stores.

Upon completion of the Aileron-Rudder Interconnect experiments, NASA began another series of tests during 1986 to investigate the airflow characteristics of variable sweep wings. The program was called the Variable Sweep Flight Test Experiment program. The experiment involved the installation of special wing coverings that would alter the airflow over the wing. It was expected that data gained from the experiment would aid in the design of future small jet transport aircraft. The modifications were done in conjunction with NASA's Langley Research Center and the Boeing Commercial Airplane Company, Seattle, Washington.

The covering, or wing glove, was designed to smooth the airflow over the wing and lead to more fuel efficient flight at high subsonic and transonic speeds. The glove was installed over the leading edge and upper surface of the wing.

The goal of the NASA and Boeing researchers was to gain information on the airflow close to the surface of the wing, known as the boundary layer. The test results were added to a data base available to aircraft designers to draw upon as they planned smaller commercial jet transport aircraft. The F-14 Tomcat was chosen to perform the tests since it had variable sweep wings and an aircraft was readily available on loan from the Navy.

An F-14A (BuNo 159834) was fitted with a glove made of fiberglass/foam composite of about one half an inch thick. A layer of fiberglass was applied to the wing, then a foam core, then several additional layers of fiberglass. Measuring devices were embedded in the glove during the manufacturing process so that a smooth surface was maintained for natural laminar airflow.

The flight test program was conducted in two phases, both at subsonic and transonic speeds, using different wing gloves and with the wings swept at varying degrees from 20 to 35 degrees. The first phase of the flight test program included twenty flights using a glove that simulated the F-14's actual airflow. This provided a base line data base for comparison once the second phase of the program began.

During the second phase, wing gloves were specially designed for speeds of .7 Mach (approximately 450 miles per hour) and .8 Mach (525 mph). Preliminary test results indicated the wing coverings, which basically smoothed out the normal wing airflow, achieved more laminar at higher wing sweep angles that the standard F-14 wing. Video from a chase aircraft gave researchers a close up look at the actual airflow over the wing, made possible by the use of liquid crystals imbedded in the surface of the gloves.

Once the tests were completed during the Fall of 1987, the aircraft was reconfigured to F-14A standards and returned to the Navy for use in the fleet.

F-14A prototype, aircraft number 1X (BuNo 157991) was loaned to NASA's Ames-Dryden Flight Research Facility at Edwards AFB, California. The aircraft was used to conduct tests of a new control system known as the Aileron-Rudder Interconnect (ARI) system, designed to coordinate turns, prevent wing rock and resist spins at high angle of attack flight conditions. (NASA)

The ARI modifications included a set of moveable canards mounted on the nose section and software changes to the aircraft's basic analog flight control system. The canards, when not in use, were hydraulically folded flush along the side of the nose. (Grumman)

The wing gloves fitted to this F-14A (BuNo 159834) were made of fiberglass. The starboard wing glove smooths out the airflow and has sensors implanted in it. The port wing was unchanged to be used as a data base constant on the characteristics of a standard F-14 wing. (NASA)

During testing, NASA and Navy pilots reported that angles approaching 70 degrees could be flown with the aircraft still flying forward, the only lift coming from the fuselage. Flight testing of the Aileron-Rudder Interconnect (ARI) commenced during June of 1985 and was completed by 9 August 1985. (NASA)

F-14D

During November of 1987, a highly modified F-14A took off from Grumman's Calverton facility. Although externally it appeared to be a standard F-14A, the aircraft (side number 501, BuNo 161865) carried the radar, avionics and digital instrumentation intended for use in the F-14D Super Tomcat program. The F-14D program was envisioned by both the Navy and Grumman as a way of providing the Navy with a state-of-the-art interceptor/fighter at substantial savings.

The F-14D Super Tomcat is basically an F-14A (Plus) updated with advanced digital avionics, instrumentation, and an improved radar. Externally, the F-14D differs from the F-14A (Plus) in the use of a dual optical/electronics chin pod which houses both the standard TCS system and an Infrared Search and Track System (IRSTS) and the deletion of the wing glove ECM fairings. Under the terms of the development/production contract signed in July of 1984, aircraft beginning with Grumman Fabrication number 596 (BuNo 163412), production block 155, will have the updates and carry the designation F-14D.

One important part of the F-14D Super Tomcat program is the Hughes AN/APG-71 radar. With high speed digital processing, this radar offers a six fold improvement in information processing over the current Hughes AWG-9 system. The AN/APG-71 radar has monopulse angle tracking and a digital scan control. The monopulse technique locates the target precisely within the radar beam while the system retains its look-down, shoot-down pulse Doppler scan/track capability. The system can track up to twenty-four targets, while guiding six missiles to their individual targets at an engagement range of over 100 miles. Target altitudes may vary from 80 to 80,000 feet.

The avionics upgrade will replace the older analog type equipment with state-of-the-art digital electronics equipment. The majority of the avionics fitted to the F-14D will be compatible with the equipment installed in the latest variants of the F/A-18 as well as the AV-8B. Other avionics improvements will include two AYK-14 mission computers, programmable digital controls and displays, an ASN-139 digital inertial navigation system, a digital stores management system and an infrared search and track system (IRSTS) housed in the same pod as the television camera set (TCS). A Tactical Data Recording System (TDRS) is installed in conjunction with the TCS (the TDRS is basically an onboard video cassette recorder (VCR) tied to the TCS). The dual pod was developed by General Electric/Martin Marietta and was first test flown on the F-14B (BuNo 157986) prototype as part o the F-14A (Plus) program.

The other items in the F-14D update include: an ALR-67 Radar Warning Receiver, an ALQ-165 Airborne Self-Protection Jammer, the Joint Tactical Information Distribution System (JTIDS) and the Naval Aircrew Common Escape System (NACES). The JTIDS is a secure fighter to fighter data link for both voice and radar information. The system allows one F-14D to pass radar information to one or more F-14Ds so that these aircraft could remain radar silent. Another advantage is that other aircraft in the vicinity such as F/A-18s or E-2Cs could receive radar information while operating their radars in a standby mode (not transmitting). Alternatively, the F-14D can receive data link information from the E-2C while remaining radar silent.

The (NACES) system is the Martin-Baker Mk 14 zero-launch ejection seat. This seat is equipped with an electronic sequencer that automatically adjusts the seat's operation to take into account the aircraft's speed and altitude at the precise moment of ejection.

The F-14D is cleared to carry a number of advanced air-to-air and air-to-ground weapons, including the Hughes AIM-120 Advanced Medium Range Air-to-Air Missile (AMRAAM) which is currently scheduled to replace the AIM-7 Sparrow medium range

missile. The AMRAAM is capable of being launched at an enemy aircraft beyond visual range and receive midcourse targeting information updates from the launch aircraft via data link. In the terminal phase, the AMRAAM's on board radar seeker guides it independently to the target without further assistance from the launch aircraft.

The AIM-120 is one third the weight of an AIM-7 and has a fifty pound blast-fragment warhead with a "smart" fuse. It has a look-down, shoot-down capability and can be launched at any target aspect angle throughout the flight envelope of the launching aircraft. The AIM-120 is compatible with the same launch rail used for the AIM-7 Sparrow without modification.

Hughes Aircraft is also working on improved variants of the Phoenix air-to-air missile, under the designations AIM-54C (Plus) and AIM-54C (Plus/Advanced). The AIM-54C (Plus) will have a built in cooling capability, eliminating the need to receive cooling air from the Tomcat. The AIM-54C (Plus) also has improvements in its Electronic Counter Counter Measures (ECCM) system. Further improvements are being developed that will ease missile production and increase the weapon's launch range.

The F-14D is powered by the same General Electric F-110-GE-400 engines used in the F-14A (Plus). The GE F-110 engines increase available thrust to 56,400 pounds and provide significant improvements in operation, reliability, maintainability and fuel consumption. The GE F-110-GE-400 has over eighty percent commonality in parts with the Air Force F-110-GE-100 engine used in the F-15 and F-16, easing spare parts procurement for both services.

The F-14D is cleared for carrying air-to-ground weapons and, while this capability has always been a part of the Tomcat's weapons load, the F-14D has the improved radar and a HUD (Head Up Display) that is very similar to that used on the F/A-18 Hornet. The F-14D carries the BRU-32 bomb rack, the same bomb rack used on the F/A-18, which will greatly improve the ground attack capability of the Tomcat. This bomb rack is capable of handling all air-to-ground weapons in the Navy inventory. Additionally, the F-14D will be able to use the AGM-78 Standard Arm anti-radiation missile.

Production of the upgraded Tomcat began during March of 1990 and current plans call for twelve new production F-14Ds and the remanufacture of six low time F-14A airframes to F-14D standards during 1990. The F-14D program calls for production of a total of 127 new production F-14Ds at a rate of twelve per year and for the remanufacture of 400 F-14As to F-14D standards, resulting in an all F-14D fleet by 1998.

This F-14A was used as the full scale development aircraft for the F-14D program. The Tomcat, side number 501 (BuNo 161865) made its first flight from the Grumman Calverton Development Test Center during November of 1987. The aircraft was a standard F-14A with F-14D radar, avionics and instrument panels. (Grumman)

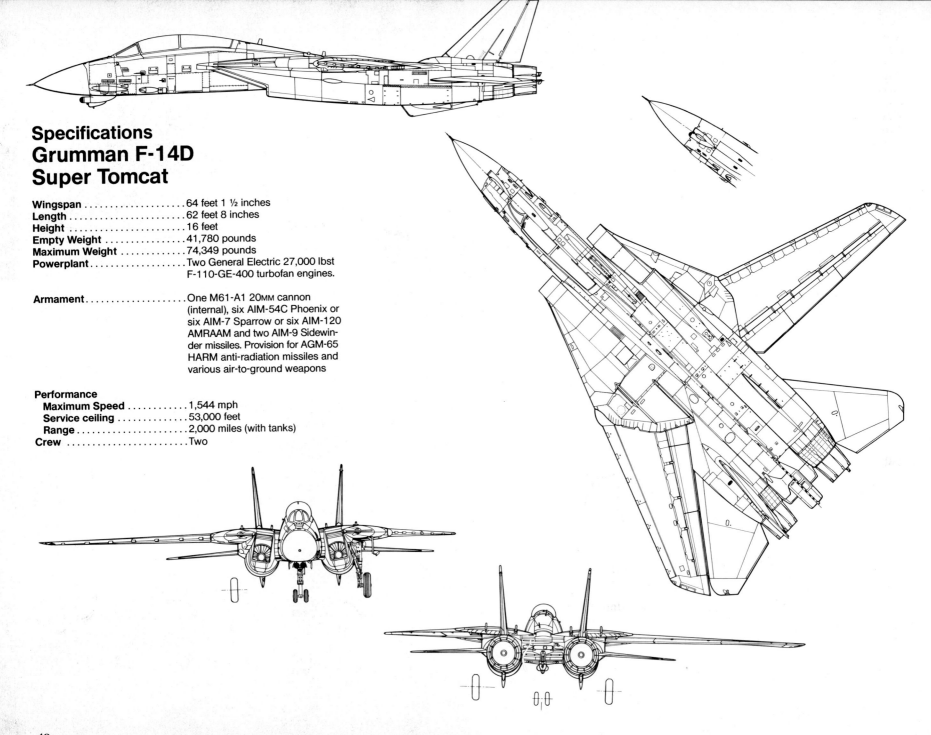

Specifications
Grumman F-14D
Super Tomcat

Wingspan . . . . 64 feet 1 ½ inches
Length . . . . 62 feet 8 inches
Height . . . . 16 feet
Empty Weight . . . . 41,780 pounds
Maximum Weight . . . . 74,349 pounds
Powerplant . . . . Two General Electric 27,000 lbst
                                            F-110-GE-400 turbofan engines.

Armament . . . . One M61-A1 20ᴍᴍ cannon
                                            (internal), six AIM-54C Phoenix or
                                            six AIM-7 Sparrow or six AIM-120
                                            AMRAAM and two AIM-9 Sidewin-
                                            der missiles. Provision for AGM-65
                                            HARM anti-radiation missiles and
                                            various air-to-ground weapons

Performance
  Maximum Speed . . . . 1,544 mph
  Service ceiling . . . . 53,000 feet
  Range . . . . 2,000 miles (with tanks)
Crew . . . . Two

The first production F-14D rolled out at Grumman during March of 1990, on schedule with the first flight being made at the end of that month. On 18 May 1990, the first F-14A scheduled for remanufacture to F-14D standards arrived at the Grumman facility. The aircraft will begin the remanufacturing cycle on 5 June 1990 and it is expected to take some fifteen months before the aircraft will have completed the program. A second F-14A is due at Grumman during September.

Current production schedules call for the F-14D Tomcat to be produced through 1995 (including rebuilds) and it is expected that the Navy will be flying the Tomcat well into the 21st Century.

Dual Chin Pod

F-14A (Plus)

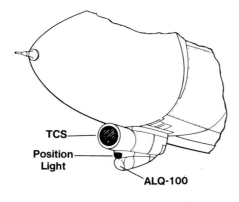

TCS

Position Light

ALQ-100

F-14D

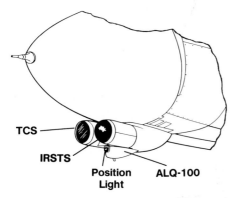

TCS

IRSTS

Position Light

ALQ-100

The first production F-14D Super Tomcat on the ramp at Grumman during March of 1990. The F-14D differs externally from the F-14A (Plus) in the addition of the dual TCS/IRSTS pod under the nose and the deletion of the wing glove ECM fairings. (Grumman)

The TCS portion of the dual TCS/IRSTS chin pod has a cover in place over the lens to protect it. F-14D production is scheduled to run through 1995 and will involve both new production aircraft and the remanufacture of F-14As to F-14D standards. (Grumman)

Great equipment and units of the 20th century —

Land,   Sea,   and Air.

2022

4002

1100

the "in action" series from squadron signal.